D1069285

# *THE NEW EROTICISM*

---

*Theories, Vogues and Canons*

# THE NEW Eroticism

*Theories, Vogues and Canons*

*Edited by*

PHILIP NOBILE

RANDOM HOUSE | NEW YORK

Copyright © 1970 by Philip Nobile

All rights reserved under International and Pan-American Copyright Conventions. Published in the United States by Random House, Inc., New York, and simultaneously in Canada by Random House of Canada Limited, Toronto.

Library of Congress Catalog Card Number: 70–102319

Manufactured in the United States of America
by H. Wolff, New York

2 4 6 8 9 7 5 3

FIRST EDITION

Acknowledgment is gratefully extended to the following for permission to reprint from their works:

*The Antioch Review:* From "The Pleasures of Commodity, or How to Make the World Safe for Pornography," by Peter Michaelson, to be published in *The Aesthetics of Pornography*, by Herder and Herder, in 1971.

Atheneum Publishers: From *Language and Silence: Essays on Language, Literature, and the Inhuman*, by George Steiner. Copyright © 1965 by George Steiner.

Basic Books, Inc.: From *The Ways of the Will*, by Leslie H. Farber. Copyright © 1966 by Leslie H. Farber.

Beacon Press: From *Eros and Civilization*, by Herbert Marcuse. Copyright © 1955, 1966 by the Beacon Press.

George Braziller, Inc.: From *Angel in Armor*, by Ernest Becker. Copyright © 1969 by Ernest Becker.

Curtis Brown Ltd.: From *Dirty Books Can Stay*, by Kenneth Tynan. Copyright © 1968 by Kenneth Tynan. First published in *Esquire*.

Enslow Publishing Corporation: "Screwed, Blewed, and Tattooed," by Joe Mancini, and "Rock 'n' Sex," by Cris Hodenfield, from *New York Scenes*. Copyright © 1969 by Enslow Publishing Corporation. All rights reserved.

*Esquire* Magazine: "The New Homosexuality," by Tom Burke. Copyright © 1969 by Esquire, Inc.

*The Humanist:* "The Desexualized Society," by Charles Winick, November/December, 1969.

International Famous Agency, Inc.: "Was It Good for You, Too?" by Dan Greenburg. Copyright © 1968 by Avant-Garde Media, Inc.

*Journal of Philosophy:* From "Sexual Perversion," by Thomas Nagel, Vol. LXVI, No. 1, January 16, 1969.

IPC Magazines Ltd.: "Revolution Is Puritan," by E. J. Hobsbawm; "Sex: Instinct or Appetite," by D. Wright; "The Sex Sell," by J. Bugler. These articles were first published in *New Society,* the weekly review of the social sciences, 128 Long Acre, London W.C. 2. © IPC Magazines Ltd.

William Morris Agency, Inc.: "Pop Sex," by Craig Karpel. Copyright © 1970 by Craig Karpel.

*New York Magazine:* "Here's Looking at You: Voyeurism in New York," by Dorothy Kalins. Copyright © 1969 by New York Magazine Co.

*Psychology Today* Magazine: "Nudity," by Paul Bindrim, June 1969. Copyright © 1969 by Communication/Research/Machines, Inc.

*Ramparts* Magazine: "Understanding Orgasm," by Susan Lydon. Copyright © 1968 by Ramparts Magazine, by permission of the Editors.

Virginia Rice: "Paydirt: Notes on the Sex Explosion," by Robert Craft. Copyright ©1969 by Robert Craft.

Wesleyan University Press: From *Life Against Death,* by Norman O. Brown. Copyright © 1959 by Wesleyan University.

# *ACKNOWLEDGMENTS*

I thank the contributors to this book, especially Craig Karpel, who wrote directly for it; and John Heidenry and Jonathan Eisen for bringing certain materials to my attention. But most of all, I remember Alice Mayhew, my editor.

P. N.

THIS BOOK IS FOR

*Jeffrey Obler*

*and*

*Ron Bittel*

# CONTENTS

# *THE NEW EROTICISM*

---

## *Theories, Vogues and Canons*

# *INTRODUCTION*

There is no effective sexual calculus, no social science to measure sexual change. This predicament allows for gross exaggeration and exaggeration of the gross. Sudden shifts in the erotic crust are considered permanent formations; guerilla actions are prematurely crested on the wave of the future. Yet the available evidence on the so-called sex revolution seems purely circumstantial—Kinsey's polls, Masters' measurements, *Portnoy's Complaint,* flavored douches, *Playboy* philosophy, gay liberation, ascending defloration rates, Helen Gurley Brown, naked therapy, off-Broadway balling, "X" movies, the Pill, Joe Namath's sportsmanlike satyriasis and much, much more. Indeed, these departures partake of the rebellion, but whether they have violently overthrown our sexual government requires proof beyond the fact of their existence.

That sort of proof is mighty hard to find. For sex resides more in the psyche than in the genitals. Sex revolution means a revolution in consciousness, in self-understanding. Some regional outposts have fallen, to be sure, but we have not yet heard the final reports from the heart of the country.

The preliminary results are in, however. By pulling together recent writings on the matter of sex, this reader puts a fix on the new eroticism. The point of view moves between theory and practice, advocacy and dissent, tragedy and farce.

In *Life Against Death* and *Eros and Civilization,*

Norman O. Brown and Herbert Marcuse fruitfully reinterpret Freud, resurrecting the body and abolishing repression. Their original probes into the erotic layers of man and society enlarge the ground of speculation and experiment. Both Brown's "The Self and the Other: Narcissus" and Marcuse's "Sexuality into Eros" are manifestoes for a radical change in consciousness. Although none of the succeeding essays can be traced to these sources, all of them can be tested against their prophecy. E. J. Hobsbawm exposes the egregious equation between political and sexual revolution, often mistakenly attributed to Brown and Marcuse, in "Revolution Is Puritan."

The rise of abnormal psychology has made perversion a household word. In "Everyman as Pervert," Ernest Becker appropriately suggests a universal application of fetishism. Thomas Nagel's psychological analysis of human sexuality, in "Sexual Perversion," yields a clear horizon in which to view the more recent behavioral adaptations reported by Dorothy Kalins in "Voyeurism in New York," by Tom Burke in "The New Homosexuality," by Paul Bindrim in "Naked Therapy," and by Joe Mancini in "Body Painting: The Youngest Profession."

Apropos literature, George Steiner's "Night Words: High Pornography and Human Privacy" and Kenneth Tynan's "Dirty Books Can Stay" ably carry on the pornography debate from opposite corners. *Playboy* magazine, another linear manifestation of commodity sex, gets the business from Peter Michaelson in "How to Make the World Safe for Pornography." Philip Nobile tells the saga of New York's most successful sex newspaper in "Inside *Screw*." To close treatment of the printed media, Jeremy Bugler's "The Sex Sell" records some case studies in the eroticization of British advertising.

The performing arts are highly visible and quite willing victims of creeping sex. Robert Craft's crosscountry comments in "Paydirt: Notes on the Sex Explosion" cover the topless girls of Hollywood, *Oh! Calcutta!* in New York, and great tracts of territory in between. Whether the ultimate embrace as simulated in *Che* ought to come under the protocols of entertainment is discussed by Ross Wetzsteon in "Staged Sexuality." "Sex Rock Symbolism" by Cris Hodenfield describes the erogenous iconography of rock music. And Craig Karpel pushes the parasexual to its weirdest conclusions in "Pop Sex."

Proceeding from the proposition that unexamined love is not worth making, much philosophizing has been expended on the act of intercourse. A dismal view of the decline of libido is taken by Charles Winick in "The Desexualized Society." Dan Greenburg lampoons the sex-lab technique in "Was It Good for You, Too?" Two interpretations clash on female orgasm: Susan Lydon's "Liberating Woman's Orgasm" and Leslie Farber's "The Traditional O."

Derek Wright puts a seemly end to the continuum with "Sex: Instinct or Appetite?" by arguing for a stronger connection between sex and affection.

This reader does not seek the last word. Gaps will be sighted and some of the trails overlap. But this is as it should be. Neither the new nor the erotic lend themselves to systematization. Nonetheless the procession of articles rallies around a single proposition—that sex is, more than we imagine, an exceedingly human enterprise. And such is the stuff of revolution.

*Philip Nobile*

*Norman O. Brown*

---

# *THE SELF AND THE OTHER: NARCISSUS*

The human family is distinguished from the animal family by a prolongation of the period in which the infant is protected from the harsh realities of life by parental care. In this sheltered situation, the erotic potentialities of human nature blossom, but blossom in an unearthly atmosphere divorced from the realities of human life. Hence this early blossoming of the erotic life must succumb to repression when it finally confronts the reality principle. But though it is repressed, or rather because it is repressed, this early experience of love stays with us as the immortal dream of love, as an indestructible demand of human nature, as the source of our restless discontent. The infantile experience to which our dreams return is an experience of pleasure, so that a return to the pleasure principle is an indestructible demand of human nature. But is a return to the pleasure principle all that human nature demands? From the Freudian point of view this question is the same as to ask whether infantile sexuality involves anything over and beyond pleasure.

Normal adult genital sexuality, both at the sensual level of physical intercourse and at the sublimated level of being in love, indicates that the sexual instinct seeks, over and beyond bodily pleasure, some appropriate form of union with objects in the world. But the pattern of normal adult sexuality can be no clue to the essential nature of the erotic desires of mankind. If we ask what relation to objects in the world is contained in the pattern of infantile sexuality, then we must take as our point of departure Freud's repeated assertions that infantile sexuality follows two paths of finding objects in the world, exhibits two modes of relating itself or binding itself to objects in the world.

The terms he uses most frequently to designate these two relations are "identification" and "object-choice." He defines identification as the desire to be like another object, and object-choice as the desire to possess another object; he usually writes as if identification is the mode in which children love their fathers, while object-choice is the mode in which they love their mothers.[1] It is through its natural propensity to make identifications and object-choices that Eros constructs the family, which in turn is the model for all social organization. And it is by making identifications with his parents that the child absorbs and makes his own their moral standards (the super-ego), so that through its propensity for identification Eros is the fountainhead of morality.

To understand the Freudian categories of identification and object-choice, we must go behind them and call for an explanation of why love of objects in the world takes these two forms and only these two. After all, it is not self-evident that love should turn out to be on the one hand a desire to be like, and on the other hand a desire to possess.

Starting from the axiom that the love of objects in the world is modeled on the primal love of the child for the mother, Freud claims that the child's relation to the mother is first and foremost a relation of dependence on the mother for survival; the path to the mother is established first of all by elementary economic needs. In the terminology of Freud's earliest pair of basic instincts, the sexual instinct follows a path to an object marked out for it by the self-preservation instinct. Freud therefore calls object-choice, modeled on this primal pattern of love of the mother, anaclitic, i.e., "leaning up against" the non-sexual instinct of self-preservation. This anaclitic character of object-choice—its connection with self-preservation, economic need, and dependence—explains why its characteristic aim is to possess its object. Quite distinct from anaclitic object-choice, and distinctly traceable not only in the neuroses and in the sexual perversions but also in the normal erotic attitudes of woman, Freud finds another pattern of choice in which the infantile model of the object is not the mother but the subject himself. The subject wants to love himself and satisfies his self-love circuitously either by loving an object like himself or by finding an object which loves him as he loves himself. Relating this second type of love to the child's general love of himself and his own body, Freud calls this second relation to objects narcissistic. Thus in some of his writings he uses the terms "narcissistic object-choice" and "anaclitic object-choice," corresponding to his later terminology of "identification" and "true object-choice" (or "object-cathexis"). Summarizing the distinction, Freud says that the human being has originally two sexual objects: himself and the woman who tends him.[2]

Freud's distinction between identification and object-choice, or between narcissistic and anaclitic object-choices, does not survive close examination. He is unable to maintain consistently the correlation of identification with love of the father and object-choice with love of the mother, and has to speak of anaclitic relations with the father and identifications with the mother.[3] But the fundamental issue is not confusion in the application of these categories, but confusion in the categories themselves. Close examination of Freud's own premises and arguments suggests that there is only one loving relationship to objects in the world, a relation of being-one-with-the-world which, though closer to Freud's narcissistic relation (identification), is also at the root of his other category of possessive love (object-choice).

If love seeks only identification with objects in the world, then possessiveness is not an essential feature of love. Our criticism is directed against Freud's notion of "true object-cathexis" as an irreducible desire to possess the beloved. The very fact that "true object-cathexis" is fundamentally anaclitic should make us suspicious of its integrity as a mode of loving. For to be anaclitic means that love follows not its own path but one marked out for it by economic needs, the fact of dependence, and the reality principle in general. Hence, as Freud himself always insisted, it is a pattern established by a fusion of the sexual instinct and the non-sexual instinct. In the phase when he assumed the two instincts to be sex and self-preservation, Freud spoke of object-choice as a manifestation of the sexual instincts leaning on the self-preservation instincts. In the phase when he assumed the two instincts to be Eros and aggression, he spoke of the inevitable aggressive component in object-choice if it is to possess its object.[4]

Furthermore, Freud's own analysis of possessive love (object-choice) and its primal model, love of the mother, shows that its erotic aim is not possession but union with the object, a union which is hardly distinguishable from his own category of identification. He derives identification from the desire for union with the world in the form of incorporation, after the primal model of the relation of the child to the mother's breast.[5] At the same time he says that incorporation of the object is the aim of normal adult loving, i.e., of object-choice.[6] Thus the distinction between object-choice and identification breaks down, both of them meeting in a project of incorporation or being-one-with-the-world, modeled on the primal relation of the child to the mother's breast. Hence Freud says that "at the very beginning, in the primitive oral phase of the individual's existence, object-cathexis and identification are hardly distinguished from each other."[7] And consistently with this, he asserts that the aim of normal adult loving is the restoration of this "primal condition in which object-libido [i.e., anaclitic object-choice] and ego-libido [i.e., narcissistic object-choice] cannot be distinguished."[8]

In Freud's later writings the importance of the early phase of dependence on the mother is increasingly emphasized, and in that context he finds it necessary to conclude that the essence of love of the mother is the need to be loved;[9] but if so, then love of the mother is essentially narcissistic, since he says that "to be loved is the aim and the satisfaction of the narcissistic object-choice."[10] One more passage from Freud's later writings shows both the breakdown of the whole distinction between anaclitic and narcissistic object-choice, and also Freud's failure explicitly to withdraw the distinction: "You remember the object-choice after the anaclitic type, which psychoanalysis talks about? The libido follows the path of the narcissistic needs, and attaches itself to the objects that ensure their satisfaction."[11]

The collapse of the distinction between identification and object-choice leaves love with one essential aim over and above pleasure, which is to become one with objects in the world. Freud himself repeatedly drew attention to the interchangeability of identification and object-choice; to explain the self-punishment in melancholia and also the self-punishing institution of the super-ego he postulated that we give up a loved object (object-choice) only on condition of making an identification with the lost object.[12] This process, which replaces an object-choice with an identification, is easier to comprehend if we abandon the notion that the two are an irreducible duality. For, as Freud says, we make the identification with the lost object by introjecting or incorporating it into the self, not really incorporating it, but incorporating it passively by making ourselves like it.

But since real incorporation of the object can be said to be the aim of object-love, the choice now appears to be not between identification and object-choice, but between active identification with the object and passive remodeling of the self so as to erect in the self a substitute for the object lost. The choice is between erotic action on the outside world (Ferenczi's "alloplastic adaptation") and passive alteration of the subject's own body and psyche as a substitute for erotic action denied (Ferenczi's "autoplastic adaptation").[13] This distinction is, I think, what Freud is driving at in the following obscure formula: "The return of the libido from the object to the ego and its transformation into narcissism makes a representation of a happy love; and conversely, an actual happy love corresponds to the primal condition in which object-libido and ego-libido cannot be distinguished."[14]

Thus Freud's clinical analysis, corrected, points to the conclusion that Eros is fundamentally a desire for union (being one) with objects in the world. But then the clinical formulations are brought in line with the more philosophical formulations in Freud's later writings, when he assumed the existence of two basic instincts, Eros and Death. From the time that he wrote *Beyond the Pleasure Principle,* he preferred to define the aim of Eros as unification or seeking union.[15] There is an obvious affinity between this doctrine of Eros and certain intuitions adumbrated in the philosophic, poetic, and religious tradition; but as a result of his failure to discard the distinction between identification and object-choice, Freud left his doctrine of Eros as seeking union hanging in metaphysical air, divorced from his deepest analyses of concrete psychological realities. Our reinterpretation is intended to open the way for an analysis of the concrete psychological realities in terms of a desire for union.

The aim of Eros is union with objects outside the self; and at the same time Eros is fundamentally narcissistic, self-loving. How can a fundamentally narcissistic orientation lead to union with objects in the world? The abstract antinomy of Self and Other in love can be overcome if we return to the concrete reality of pleasure and to the fundamental definition of sexuality as the pleasurable activity of the body, and think of loving as the relation of the ego to its sources of pleasure. Narcissistic love is fundamentally a desire for pleasurable activity of one's own body. Our problem then is: How does the desire for pleasurable activity of one's own body lead to other bodies?

The answer is contained in Freud's doctrine of the peculiar ego-structure, the sense of one's relation to the outside world, which is developed in infancy and which, like the rest of infantile sexuality, is repressed but never abandoned in the adult. In the unreal, protected situation of human infancy, the infant develops an unreal sense of reality. Reality is his mother, that is to say, love and pleasure; infantile sexuality affirms the union of the self with a whole world of love and pleasure.

In technical Freudian terminology, the infant develops a pure pleasure-ego instead of a reality-ego, a pure pleasure-ego which absorbs into identity with itself the sources of its pleasure, its world, its mother.[16] Hence "the ego-feeling we are aware of now is thus only a shrunken vestige of a far more extensive feeling—a feeling which embraced the universe and expressed an inseparable connection of the ego with the external world." [17] But the primal experience of union of the self with a world of love and pleasure sets the pattern for all human love, so that "when later on an object manifests itself as a source of pleasure, it becomes loved, but also incorporated into the ego."[18] Hence "an actual happy love corresponds to the primal condition in which object-libido and ego-libido cannot be distinguished." Freud summarizes the development of love thus: "Love originates in the capacity of the ego to satisfy some of its instincts autoerotically through the obtaining of organ-pleasure. It is primarily narcissistic, is then transferred to those objects which have been incorporated in the ego, now much extended, and expresses the motor striving of the ego after these objects as sources of pleasure."[19] Thus the human libido is essentially narcissistic, but it seeks a world to love as it loves itself.

It is the human ego that carries the search for a world to love: or rather this project, in the unconscious stratum of the ego, guides human consciousness in its restless search for an object that can satisfy its love, as in St. Augustine: "I did not yet love, and I loved to love; I sought what I might love, in love with loving." Freud says not only that the human ego-feeling once embraced the whole world, but also that Eros drives the ego to recover that feeling: "The development of the ego consists in a departure from primal narcissism and results in a vigorous attempt to recover it."[20] In primal narcissism the self is at one with a world of love and pleasure; hence the ultimate aim of the human ego is to reinstate what Freud calls "limitless narcissism"[21] and find itself once more at one with the whole world in love and pleasure. The erotic energy in the ego is in the (unconscious) pure pleasure-ego project; and hence the pure pleasure-ego is in conflict with the reality-ego, until reality and pleasure can really meet and create what Ferenczi called "the erotic sense of reality." Eros, as a force in the human ego, seeks to *affirm* a world of love and pleasure: "Affirmation, as being a substitute for union, belongs to Eros."[22]

The principle of erotic exuberance needs to be incorporated into Freud's doctrine of the narcissistic Eros. In technical psychoanalytical terms, Freud recognizes that libido goes out to objects from what he calls a "narcissistic reservoir," [23] but is not clear why that reservoir must overflow. The nearest Freud comes to answering this question is in the essay "On Narcissism" (1914):[24]

> Whence does that necessity arise that urges our mental life to pass on beyond the limits of narcissism and to attach the libido to objects? The answer which would follow from our line of thought would once more be that we are so impelled when the cathexis of the ego with libido exceeds a certain degree. A strong egoism is a protection against disease, but in the last resort we must begin to love in order that we may not fall ill, and must fall ill if, in consequence of frustration, we cannot love. Somewhat after this fashion does Heine conceive of the psychogenesis of the Creation.

But later writings show Freud's feeling that he does not fully comprehend the attachment of libido to objects. In the essay "On Transience" (1915), speaking of mourning, he says: "But why it is that this detachment of libido from its objects should be such a painful process is a mystery to us and we have not hitherto been able to frame any hypothesis to account for it." [25] And in a footnote in *Civilization and Its Discontents* (1930)—omitted in the English translation—Freud poses the limits of narcissism as a still unsolved problem: "A consideration of the possibilities of human happiness should not neglect to take into account the relative proportions of narcissism and object-libido. One would like to know what it means for the economy of the libido to be essentially dependent on oneself." [26]

One can see Freud's thought inhibited by a conception of Self and Other as mutually exclusive alternatives. The image of Narcissus in myth and poetry points in another direction: Narcissus needs a pool, a mirror, in which to see himself. And, in the mysticism of Boehme, the psychogenesis of Creation is God's need for "self-reflection" (*Selbstabbildung*) and for a mirror (*Spiegel*) in which to see himself.[27] Along these lines Freud's narcissism would have the need for the Other more deeply grounded: narcissism, like Narcissus, would be a fountain of play and of erotic exuberance. Nietzsche's Zarathustra says, "I love him whose soul is overfull so that he forgets himself and all things are in him"; and also, "His word pronounced *selfishness* blessed, the wholesome healthy selfishness that wells from a powerful soul—from a powerful soul to which belongs the high body, beautiful, triumphant, refreshing, around which everything becomes a mirror—the supple, persuasive body, the dancer whose parable and epitome is the self-enjoying soul." [28]

The psychoanalytical method seeks to connect the dreams of metaphysics with the physiology of dreams; the physiological basis of the narcissistic Eros and of the pure pleasure-ego project is the relation of the infant to the mother's breast. "The suckling of the child at the mother's breast has become a model for every love relation. Object-finding is really a re-finding." [29] "The state of being in love results from the fulfillment of infantile conditions of love . . . whatever fulfills this condition of love becomes idealized." [30] "The desire to suck includes within it the desire for the mother's breast, which is therefore the first object of sexual desire; I cannot convey to you any adequate idea of the importance of this first object in determining every later object adopted, of the profound influence it exerts, through transformation and substitution, upon the most distant fields of mental life." [31]

Here again Freud is only seeing face to face what religious and poetic mysticism has divined darkly and expressed symbolically in the cult of the Madonna and Child. Evelyn Underhill's book on mysticism is prefaced by this quotation from Coventry Patmore: "The Babe sucking its mother's breast, and the Lover returning, after twenty years' separation, to his home and food in the same bosom, are the types and princes of Mystics." *Das Ewig-*

*Weibliche* draws us on: Faust, the incarnation of our restless discontent, achieves final salvation, which is also the end of restlessly striving Faustian man, in his reunion with *das Ewig-Weibliche* in a cloud of mother-figures led by the Mater Gloriosa who is Virgin, Mother, and Queen, so that "Eros may rule, for he began all." [32]

At the mother's breast, in Freudian language, the child experiences that primal condition, forever after idealized, "in which object-libido and ego-libido cannot be distinguished";[33] in philosophic language, the subject-object dualism does not corrupt the blissful experience of the child at the mother's breast. But the subject-object dualism is not the only dualism which besets our adult interaction with the world; and conversely, the primal childhood experience, according to Freud, is idealized because it is free from all dualisms. If therefore we think of man as that species of animal which has the historical project of recovering his own childhood, psychoanalysis suggests the eschatological proposition that mankind will not put aside its sickness and its discontent until it is able to abolish every dualism.

In psychoanalytical theory, the dualisms besetting human interaction with the world stem not from the subject-object relation but from the dualism of instincts inside the subject. Throughout the evolution of Freud's thought, Eros always has an antagonist. In his earlier theory the antagonist is self-preservation, or the ego-instinct (more colloquially, hunger); in his later theory the antagonist is the death or aggressive instinct. The whole theory of Eros therefore must hang somewhat in the air until we have examined Eros' antagonist. But we can introduce in advance the Freudian theorem that the instinctual life of man starts from a primitive undifferentiated fusion of the two instincts—a fusion in which they are not mutually antagonistic—and, insofar as it is fixated to childhood, seeks to restore the instinctual fusion. The relation of the child to the mother's breast remains our ideal because it represents such an instinctual fusion. When Freud was thinking of the dualism of the sexual and self-preservation instincts (love and hunger), he coined the term "anaclitic" (i.e., "leaning up against") to describe the relation between the two instincts in the child at the breast, where the first satisfaction of the sexual instinct is simultaneously the first satisfaction of the self-preservation instinct (or ego instinct): "The first auto-erotic sexual gratifications are experienced in connection with vital functions in the service of self-preservation. The sexual instincts are at the outset supported upon the ego-instincts." [34] We have already argued that Freud was wrong in trying to present anaclitic love as a second mode of loving, distinct from narcissistic love; the primal anaclitic situation, which, according to Freud, remains our ideal of love, does not represent a distinct mode of loving but a fusion of the erotic with the nonerotic, specifically economic (self-preservation, hunger) needs and satisfactions.

But according to psychoanalysis this state of instinctual fusion remains our unconscious ideal; and on the other hand civilization makes antagonistic opposites out of economics and love, work and play. Psychoanalysis thus suggests that mankind will not cease from discontent and sickness until the antinomy of economics and love, work and play, is overcome. We are back once more to the utopian dreams of Fourier and to his serious exploration of the possibility of realizing the goal of *travail attrayant,* pleasurable work.

In Freud's writings after 1920 the antithesis of the sexual and self-preservation instincts is replaced by the antithesis of Eros and what Freud called either the aggressive or the destructive or the death instinct. The fundamental polarity in human nature, in Freud's later writings, is not hunger and love, but love and hate, love and aggression, love and the will to power. But the primal experience of satisfaction, which retains humanity's unconscious allegiance, is free not only from the antinomy of work and play but also from the ambivalence of love and hate. Freud, misled by his metaphysical bias toward dualism often speaks as if the ambivalence of love and hate were a fundamental fact of human nature, present in the child from the start.[35] But when he is not theorizing but simply analyzing the facts, he says that in the earliest phase "there is no ambivalence in the relation to the object, i.e., the mother's breast." [36]

There is a technical point at issue here in the psychoanalytical theory of the stages through which infantile sexuality passes on the way to genital organization. The first stage, the oral stage—the stage in which the child's chief zone of pleasure is the mouth at the mother's breast—is subdivided into a first oral phase distinct from a second phase, the second phase being "distinguished by the onset of biting activities," and therefore being called "the oral-sadistic phase." [37] The appearance of aggressive biting activities marks the first emergence of the ambivalence of love and hate: hence Abraham calls the first oral stage "pre-ambivalent." [38]

Thus the ambivalence of love and hate is not an innate datum of human nature (and one of the grounds for Freud's pessimism disappears). Or rather, Freud's own doctrine that man in his unconscious keeps his allegiance to the primal experience of satisfaction at the mother's breast requires us to say that man unconsciously seeks to abolish the ambivalence of love and hate. And in fact Freud's later writings attribute to the human ego a basic tendency to "reconcile," "synthesize," "unify" the dualisms and conflicts with which the human being is beset;[39] Abraham sets the goal of achieving a "post-ambivalent" stage;

Ferenczi calls for a "fresh instinctual fusion." [40] But the possibility of post-ambivalent instinctual refusion must remain hypothetical until we have examined the cause of the ambivalence and the nature of Eros' instinctual antagonist.

[1] *Group Psychology and the Analysis of Ego* (hereafter cited as GP), tr. J. Strachey. (International Psycho-Analytical Library, no. 6) London, Vienna: The International Psycho-Analytical Press, 1922, 60–62; *New Introductory Lectures on Psychoanalysis* (hereafter cited as NIL), tr. W. J. H. Sprott. (International Psycho-Analytical Library, no. 24) London: Hogarth Press and The Institute of Psycho-Analysis, 1933, 86.

[2] *Collected Papers* (hereafter cited as CP and volume number), ed. J. Riviere & J. Strachey. International Psycho-Analytical Library, no. 7–10, 37) New York, London: The International Psycho-Analytical Press, 1924–50, vol. 4, 44–45; *The Basic Writings of Sigmund Freud* (hereafter cited as BW), tr. & ed. A. A. Brill. New York: The Modern Library, 1938, 614 and note; *A General Introduction to Psycho-Analysis* (hereafter cited as GI), tr. J. Riviere. New York: Perma Giants, 1953. Copyright 1935 by Edward L. Bernays, 433–34.

[3] CP IV, 47; *The Ego and the Id* (hereafter cited as EI), tr. J. Riviere. (International Psycho-Analytical Library, no. 12) London: Hogarth Press and The Institution of Psycho-Analysis, 1927, 40–44.

[4] CP V, 281.

[5] GP 60–61; NIL 86.

[6] CP IV, 78–81.

[7] EI 35.

[8] CP IV, 57. Cf. EI 36 and note; GP 73–76.

[9] *Inhibitions, Symptoms and Anxiety* (hereafter cited as ISA), tr. A. Strachey. (International Psycho-Analytical Library, no. 28) London: Hogarth Press and The Institute of Psycho-Analysis, 1936, 105–10, 117, 122, 140; NIL 115–16.

[10] CP IV, 55; NIL 170.

[11] *The Future of an Illusion* (hereafter cited as FI), tr. W. D. Robson-Scott. (International Psycho-Analytical Library, no.

15) London: Hogarth Press and The Institute of Psycho-Analysis, 1928, 41.

[12] CP IV, 152–70; NIL 86.

[13] EI 36; ISA 27–28; F. Ferenczi, *Further Contributions to the Theory and Technique of Psycho-analysis.* London: Hogarth Press, 1952; (New York: Basic Books, 1952) 97, 164.

[14] CP IV, 57. Cf. BW 876.

[15] *Beyond the Pleasure Principle* (hereafter cited as BPP), tr. J. Strachey. (International Psycho-Analytical Library, ed. E. Jones, no. 4) London: Hogarth Press, 1950, 57, 68; *An Outline of Psychoanalysis* (hereafter cited as OP), tr. J. Strachey. (International Psycho-Analytical Library, no. 35) London: Hogarth Press, 1949, 6; CP V, 185, 350; *Civilization and Its Discontents* (hereafter cited as CD), tr. J. Riviere. (International Psycho-Analytical Library, ed. E. Jones, no. 17) London: Hogarth, 1930, 97, 164.

[16] CP IV, 78–79; CD 12.

[17] CD 13.

[18] CP IV, 79.

[19] CP IV, 81.

[20] CP IV, 57.

[21] CD 21.

[22] CP V, 185.

[23] EI 63; OP 8; CP IV, 350; GI 423.

[24] CP IV, 42. Cf. GI 428.

[25] CP V, 81.

[26] Freud, *Gesammelte Werke*, XIV. London: Imago Publishing Co., 1948, 443, note; cf. CD 41.

[27] Cf. E. Benz, *Der vollkommene Mensch nach Jacob Boehme.* Stuttgart: W. Kohlhammer, 1937, 9–11, 25–26, 31, 35.

[28] Walter Kaufmann, *The Portable Nietzsche.* New York: Viking Press, 1954, 128, 302.

[29] BW, 614.

[30] CP IV, 58.

[31] GI 323.

[32] Goethe, *Faust,* Part II, vs. 8479.

[33] CP IV, 57.

[34] CP IV, 44. Cf. BW 587; GI 322–23, 434; GP 60–62.

[35] BW 854; GP 61; EI 61; NIL 159; CP V, 263.

[36] NIL 129.

[37] NIL 129.

[38] K. Abraham, *Selected Papers on Psychoanalysis,* tr. D. Bryan and A. Strachey. New York: Basic Books, 1953, 481.

[39] CP II, 253, 395; ISA 33, 36, 61, 71; *Moses and Monotheism,* tr. K. Jones. (International Psycho-Analytical Library, no. 33) London: Hogarth Press and The Institute of Psycho-Analysis, 1939; (New York: Knopf, 1939) 125; CP V, 326, 337.

[40] Abraham, loc. cit.; Ferenczi, *Further Contributions,* 372.

## *Herbert Marcuse*

---

# *SEXUALITY INTO EROS*

Libido can take the road of self-sublimation only as a *social* phenomenon: as an unrepressed force, it can promote the formation of culture only under conditions which relate associated individuals to each other in the cultivation of the environment for their developing needs and facul-

---

*Editor's note:* This essay is excerpted from the chapter entitled "The Transformation of Sexuality into Eros" in Marcuse's *Eros and Civilization.* Up to this point in the chapter Marcuse has argued for the possibility of a non-repressive civilization based on a non-repressive reality principle. He tests this possibility on the "disorderly" instinct of sexuality. Departing from Freud who feared the decrease in societal constraints over sex, Marcuse welcomes the reversal of the process which keeps libido locked up for the sake of law and order. "The regression involved in this spread of the libido would first manifest itself in the reactivation of all erotogenic zones and, consequently, in a resurgence of pregenital polymorphous sexuality and in a decline of genital supremacy. The body in its entirety would become an object of cathexis, a thing to be enjoyed—an instrument of pleasure."

There is more to instinctual liberation than mere release, however. The libido is actually transformed—"from sexuality constrained under genital supremacy to erotization of the entire personality. It is a spread rather than an explosion of libido—a spread over private and societal relations which bridges the gap maintained between them by a repressive reality principle."

In this way, according to Marcuse, "the free development of transformed libido within transformed institutions, while eroticizing previously tabooed zones, time, and relations, would *minimize* the manifestations of *mere* sexuality by integrating them into a far larger order, including the order of work."

ties. Reactivation of polymorphous and narcissistic sexuality ceases to be a threat to culture and can itself lead to culture-building if the organism exists not as an instrument of alienated labor but as a subject of self-realization—in other words, if socially useful work is at the same time the transparent satisfaction of an individual need. In primitive society, this organization of work may be immediate and "natural"; in mature civilization, it can be envisaged only as the result of liberation. Under such conditions, the impulse to "obtain pleasure from the zones of the body" may extend to seek its objective in lasting and expanding libidinal relations because this expansion increases and intensifies the instinct's gratification. Moreover, nothing in the nature of Eros justifies the notion that the "extension" of the impulse is confined to the corporeal sphere. If the antagonistic separation of the physical from the spiritual part of the organism is itself the historical result of repression, the overcoming of this antagonism would open the spiritual sphere to the impulse. The aesthetic idea of a sensuous reason suggests such a tendency. It is essentially different from sublimation in so far as the spiritual sphere becomes the "direct" object of Eros and remains a libidinal object: there is a change neither in energy nor in aim.

The notion that Eros and Agape may after all be one and the same—not that Eros is Agape but that Agape is Eros—may sound strange after almost two thousand years of theology. Nor does it seem justifiable to refer to Plato as a defender of this identification—Plato who himself introduced the repressive definition of Eros into the household of Western culture. Still, the *Symposium* contains the clearest celebration of the sexual origin and substance of the spiritual relations. According to Diotima, Eros drives the desire for one beautiful body to another and finally to all beautiful bodies, for "the beauty of one body is akin to the beauty of another," and it would be foolish "not to recognize that the beauty in every body is one and the same."[1] Out of this truly polymorphous sexuality arises the desire for that which animates the desired body: the psyche and its various manifestations. There is an unbroken ascent in erotic fulfillment from the corporeal love of one to that of the others, to the love of beautiful work and play (ἐπιϑηδεύματα), and ultimately to the love of beautiful knowledge (καλα μαϑηματα). The road to "higher culture" leads through the true love of boys (ὀρϑῶς παιδεραστειν).[2] Spiritual "procreation" is just as much the work of Eros as is corporeal procreation, and the right and true order of the Polis is just as much an erotic one as is the right and true order of love. The culture-building power of Eros *is* non-repressive sublimation: sexuality is neither deflected from nor blocked in its objective; rather, in attaining its objective, it transcends it to others, searching for fuller gratification.

In the light of the idea of non-repressive sublimation, Freud's definition of Eros as striving to "form living substance into ever greater unities, so that life may be prolonged and brought to higher development"[3] takes on added significance. The biological drive becomes a cultural drive. The pleasure principle reveals its own dialectic. The erotic aim of sustaining the entire body as subject-object of pleasure calls for the continual refinement of the organism, the intensification of its receptivity, the growth of its sensuousness. The aim generates its own projects of realization: the abolition of toil, the amelioration of the environment, the conquest of disease and decay, the creation of luxury. All these activities flow directly from the

---

[1] 210 B. Jowett translates, not "body," but "form."

[2] 211 B. Jowett translates: ". . . under the influence of true love."

[3] S. Freud, *Collected Papers* (London: Hogarth Press, 1950). V, 135.

pleasure principle, and, at the same time, they constitute *work* which associates individuals to "greater unities"; no longer confined within the mutilating dominion of the performance principle, they modify the impulse without deflecting it from its aim. There is sublimation and, consequently, culture; but this sublimation proceeds in a system of expanding and enduring libidinal relations, which are in themselves work relations.

The idea of an erotic tendency toward work is not foreign to psychoanalysis. Freud himself remarked that work provides an opportunity for a "very considerable discharge of libidinal component impulses, narcissistic, aggressive and even erotic." [4] We have questioned this statement [5] because it makes no distinction between alienated and nonalienated labor (between labor and work): the former is by its very nature repressive of human potentialities and therefore also repressive of the "libidinal component impulses" which may enter into work. But the statement assumes a different significance if it is seen in the context of the social psychology which Freud proposes in *Group Psychology and the Analysis of the Ego.* He suggests that "the libido props itself upon the satisfaction of the great vital needs, and chooses as its first objects the people who have a share in that process." [6] This proposition, if unfolded in its implications, comes close to vitiating Freud's basic assumption that the "struggle for existence" (that is, for the "satisfaction of the great vital needs") is *per se* anti-libidinous in so far as it necessitates the regimentation of the instinct by a constraining reality principle. It must be noted that Freud links the libido not

---

[4] *Civilization and Its Discontents* (London: Hogarth Press, 1949), p. 34 note.

[5] See Chapter 4, "The Dialectic of Civilization" in Herbert Marcuse, *Eros and Civilization* (Vintage Books, 1962).

[6] Marcuse, p. 52.

merely to the *satisfaction* of the great vital needs but to the joint human efforts to *obtain* satisfaction, i.e., to the work process:

> . . . experience has shown that in cases of collaboration libidinal ties are regularly formed between the fellow-workers which prolong and solidify the relations between them to a point beyond what is merely profitable.[7]

If this is true, then Ananke is not a sufficient cause for the instinctual constraints of civilization—and not a sufficient reason for denying the possibility of a nonrepressive libidinous culture. Freud's suggestions in *Group Psychology and the Analysis of the Ego* do more than reformulate his thesis of Eros as the builder of culture; culture here rather appears as the builder of Eros—that is to say, as the "natural" fulfillment of the innermost trend of Eros. Freud's psychology of civilization was based on the inexorable conflict between Ananke and free instinctual development. But if Ananke itself becomes the primary field of libidinal development, the contradiction evaporates. Not only would the struggle for existence not necessarily cancel the possibility of instinctual freedom; but it would even constitute a "prop" for instinctual gratification. The work relations which form the base of civilization, and thus civilization itself, would be "propped" by non-desexualized instinctual energy. The whole concept of sublimation is at stake.

The problem of work, of socially useful activity, without (repressive) sublimation can now be restated. It emerged as the problem of a change in the character of work by virtue of which the latter would be assimilated to play—the free play of human faculties. What are the instinctual preconditions for such a transformation? The most far-reaching attempt to answer this question is made by Barbara Lantos in her article "Work and the

---

[7] *Ibid.*

Instincts."[8] She defines work and play in terms of the instinctual stages involved in these activities. Play is entirely subject to the pleasure principle: pleasure is in the movement itself in so far as it activates erotogenic zones. "The fundamental feature of play is, that it is gratifying in itself, without serving any other purpose than that of instinctual gratification." The impulses that determine play are the pregenital ones: play expresses objectless autoeroticism and gratifies those component instincts which are already directed toward the objective world. Work, on the other hand, serves ends outside itself—namely, the ends of self-preservation. "To work is the active effort of the ego . . . to get from the outside world whatever is needed for self-preservation." This contrast establishes a parallelism between the organization of the instincts and that of human activity:

> Play is an aim in itself, work is the agent of self-preservation. Component instincts and auto-erotic activities seek pleasure with no ulterior consequences; genital activity is the agent of procreation. The genital organization of the sexual instincts has a parallel in the work-organization of the ego-instincts.[9]

Thus it is the purpose and not the content which marks an activity as play or work.[10] A transformation in the instinctual structure (such as that from the pregenital to the genital stage) would entail a change in the instinctual value of the human activity *regardless of its content*. For example, if work were accompanied by a reactivation of pregenital polymorphous eroticism, it would tend to become gratifying in itself without losing its *work* content. Now it is precisely such a reactivation of polymorphous eroticism

---

[8] In *International Journal of Psychoanalysis*, Vol. XXIV (1943), Parts 3 and 4, pp. 114ff.

[9] *Ibid.*, p. 117.

[10] *Ibid.*, p. 118.

which appeared as the consequence of the conquest of scarcity and alienation. The altered societal conditions would therefore create an instinctual basis for the transformation of work into play. In Freud's terms, the less the efforts to obtain satisfaction are impeded and directed by the interest in domination, the more freely the libido could prop itself upon the satisfaction of the great vital needs. Sublimation and domination hang together. And the dissolution of the former would, with the transformation of the instinctual structure, also transform the basic attitude toward man and nature which has been characteristic of Western civilization.

In psychoanalytic literature, the development of libidinal work relations is usually attributed to a "general maternal attitude as the dominant trend of a culture."[11] Consequently, it is considered as a feature of primitive societies rather than as a possibility of mature civilization. Margaret Mead's interpretation of Arapesh culture is entirely focused on this attitude:

> To the Arapesh, the world is a garden that must be tilled, not for one's self, not in pride and boasting, not for hoarding and usury, but that the yams and the dogs and the pigs and most of all the children may grow. From this whole attitude flow many of the other Arapesh traits, the lack of conflict between the old and young, the lack of any expectation of jealousy or envy, the emphasis upon co-operation.[12]

Foremost in this description appears the fundamentally different experience of the world: nature is taken, not as an object of domination and exploitation, but as a "garden" which can grow while making human beings grow. It is the attitude that experiences man and nature as joined

---

[11] Róheim, *The Origin and Function of Culture* (New York: Nervous and Mental Disease Monograph No. 69, 1943), p. 75.

[12] *Sex and Temperament in Three Primitive Societies* (New York: New American Library, 1952), p. 100.

in a non-repressive and still functioning order. We have seen how the otherwise most divergent traditions of thought converged on this idea: the philosophical opposition against the performance principle; the Orphic and Narcissistic archetypes; the aesthetic conception. But while the psychoanalytical and anthropological concepts of such an order have been oriented on the prehistorical and precivilized *past,* our discussion of the concept is oriented on the *future,* on the conditions of fully mature civilization. The transformation of sexuality into Eros, and its extension to lasting libidinal work relations, here presupposes the rational reorganization of a huge industrial apparatus, a highly specialized societal division of labor, the use of fantastically destructive energies, and the cooperation of vast masses.

The idea of libidinal work relations in a developed industrial society finds little support in the tradition of thought, and where such support is forthcoming it seems of a dangerous nature. The transformation of labor into pleasure is the central idea in Fourier's giant socialist utopia. If

> . . . l'industrie est la destination qui nous est assignée par le créateur, comment penser qu'il veuille nous y amener par la violence, et qu'il n'ait pas su mettre on jeu quelque ressort plus noble, quelqu'amorce capable de transformer les travaux en plaisirs.[13]

Fourier insists that this transformation requires a complete change in the social institutions: distribution of the social product according to need, assignment of functions according to individual faculties and inclinations, constant

[13] If "industry is the fate assigned to us by the Creator, how can one believe that he wishes to force us into it—that he does not know how to bring to bear some nobler means, some enticement capable of transforming work into pleasure." F. Armand and R. Maublanc, *Fourier: Textes Choisis* (Paris: Editions Sociales Internationales, 1937), III, 154.

mutation of functions, short work periods, and so on. But the possibility of "attractive labor" (*travail attrayant*) derives above all from the release of libidinal forces. Fourier assumes the existence of an *attraction industrielle* which makes for pleasurable cooperation. It is based on the *attraction passionnée* in the nature of man, which persists despite the opposition of reason, duty, prejudice. This *attraction passionnée* tends toward three principal objectives: the creation of "luxury, or the pleasure of the five senses"; the formation of libidinal groups (of friendship and love); and the establishment of a harmonious order, organizing these groups for work in accordance with the development of the individual "passions" (internal and external "play" of faculties).[14] Fourier comes closer than any other utopian socialist to elucidating the dependence of freedom on non-repressive sublimation. However, in his detailed blueprint for the realization of this idea, he hands it over to a giant organization and administration and thus retains the repressive elements. The working communities of the *phalanstère* anticipate "strength through joy" rather than freedom, the beautification of mass culture rather than its abolition. Work as free play cannot be subject to administration; only alienated labor can be organized and administered by rational routine. It is beyond this sphere, but on its basis, that non-repressive sublimation creates its own cultural order.

Once more, we emphasize that non-repressive sublimation is utterly incompatible with the institutions of the performance principle and implies the negation of this principle. This contradiction is the more important since post-Freudian psychoanalytic theory itself shows a marked tendency to obliterate it and to glorify repressive productivity as human self-realization. A striking example is provided by Ives Hendrick in his paper "Work and the

---

[14] *Ibid.*, II, 240ff.

Pleasure Principle."[15] He suggests that the "energy and the need to exercise the physiological organs available for work" are not provided by the libido but rather by a special instinct, the "mastery instinct." Its aim is "to control, or alter a piece of the environment . . . by the skillful use of perceptual, intellectual, and motor techniques." This drive for "integration and skillful performance" is "mentally and emotionally experienced as the need to perform work efficiently."[16] Since work is thus supposed to be itself the gratification of an instinct rather than the "temporary negation" of an instinct, work "yields pleasure" in efficient performance. Work pleasure results from the satisfaction of the mastery instinct, but "work pleasure" and libidinal pleasure usually coincide, since the ego organizations which function as work are "generally, and perhaps always, utilized concurrently for the discharge of surplus libidinal tension."[17]

As usual, the revision of Freudian theory means a retrogression. The assumption of any special instinct begs the question, but the assumption of a special "mastery instinct" does even more: it destroys the entire structure and dynamic of the "mental apparatus" which Freud has built. Moreover, it obliterates the most repressive features of the performance principle by interpreting them as gratification of an instinctual need. Work pure and simple is the chief social manifestation of the reality principle. In so far as work is conditional upon delay and diversion of instinctual gratification (and according to Freud it is), it contradicts the pleasure principle. If work pleasure and libidinal pleasure "usually coincide," then the very concept of the reality principle becomes meaningless and superfluous, and the vicissitudes of the instincts as described by Freud would at best be an abnormal development. Nor can the

[15] *Psychoanalytic Quarterly*, Vol. XII, No. 3 (1943).

[16] *Ibid.*, p. 314.

[17] *Ibid.*, p. 317.

reality principle be saved by stipulating (as Hendrick does) a work principle different from the reality principle; for if the latter does not govern work it has practically nothing to govern in the reality.

To be sure, there is work that yields pleasure in skillful performance of the bodily organs "available for work." But what kind of work, and what kind of pleasure? If pleasure is indeed in the act of working and not extraneous to it, such pleasure must be derived from the acting organs of the body and the body itself, activating the erotogenic zones or eroticizing the body as a whole; in other words, it must be libidinal pleasure. In a reality governed by the performance principle, such "libidinal" work is a rare exception and can occur only outside or at the margin of the work world—as "hobby," play, or in a directly erotic situation. The normal kind of work (socially useful occupational activity) in the prevailing division of labor is such that the individual, in working, does *not* satisfy *his* own impulses, needs, and faculties but performs a preestablished function. Hendrick, however, takes no notice of the fact of *alienated* labor, which is the predominant mode of work under the given reality principle. Certainly there can be "pleasure" in alienated labor too. The typist who hands in a perfect transcript, the tailor who delivers a perfectly fitting suit, the beauty-parlor attendant who fixes the perfect hairdo, the laborer who fulfills his quota—all may feel pleasure in a "job well done." However, either this pleasure is extraneous (anticipation of reward), or it is the satisfaction (itself a token of repression) of being well occupied, in the right place, of contributing one's part to the functioning of the apparatus. In either case, such pleasure has nothing to do with primary instinctual gratification. To link performances on assembly lines, in offices and shops with instinctual needs is to glorify dehumanization as pleasure. It is no wonder that Hendrick considers as the "sublime test of men's will to perform their work effectively" the efficient functioning of an army which has no longer any "fantasies of victory and a pleasant future," which keeps on fighting for no other reason than because it is the soldier's job to fight, and "to do the job was the only motivation that was still meaningful." [18] To say that the job must be done because it is a "job" is truly the apex of alienation, the total loss of instinctual and intellectual freedom—repression which has become, not the second, but the first nature of man.

In contrast to such aberrations, the true spirit of psychoanalytic theory lives in the uncompromising efforts to reveal the anti-humanistic forces behind the philosophy of productiveness:

> Of all things, hard work has become a virtue instead of the curse it was always advertised to be by our remote ancestors. . . . Our children should be prepared to bring their children up so they won't have to work as a neurotic necessity. The necessity to work is a neurotic symptom. It is a crutch. It is an attempt to make oneself feel valuable even though there is no particular need for one's working.[19]

---

[18] *Ibid.*, p. 324.

[19] C. B. Chisholm in the panel discussion "The Psychiatry of Enduring Peace and Social Progress," in *Psychiatry*, Vol. IX, No. 1 (1946), p. 31.

# *E. J. Hobsbawm*

---

## *REVOLUTION IS PURITAN*

The late Che Guevara would have been very surprised and acutely irritated by the discovery that his picture has now been on the cover of *Evergreen Review,* his personality the subject of an article in *Vogue,* and his name the ostensible excuse for some homosexual exhibitionism in a New York theater. We can leave *Vogue* aside. Its business is to tell women what it is fashionable to wear, to know and to talk about; its interest in Che Guevara has no more political implications than the editor's of *Who's Who.* The other two jokes, however, reflect a widespread belief that there is some sort of connection between social-revolutionary movements and permissiveness in public sexual or other personal behavior. It is about time someone pointed out that there are no good grounds for this belief.

In the first place, it ought now to be evident that conventions about what sexual behavior is permissible in public have no specific connection with systems of political rule or social and economic exploitation. (Exceptions are the rule of men over women and the exploitation of women by men which, at a guess, imply more or less strict limitations on the public behavior of the inferior sex.) Sexual "liberation" has only indirect relations with any other kind of liberation. Systems of class rule and exploitation may impose strict conventions of personal (for example, sexual) behavior in public or private, or they may not. Hindu society was not in any sense more free or egalitarian than the Welsh nonconformist community, because the one used temples to demonstrate a vast variety of sexual activities in the most tempting manner, whereas the other imposed rigid restrictions on its members, at any rate in theory. All we can deduce from this particular cultural difference is that pious Hindus who wanted to vary their sexual routine could learn to do so much more easily than pious Welshmen.

Indeed, if a rough generalization about the relation between class rule and sexual freedom is possible, it is that rulers find it convenient to encourage sexual permissiveness or laxity among their subjects if only to keep their minds off their subjection.

Nobody ever imposed sexual puritanism on slaves; quite the contrary. The sort of societies in which the poor are strictly kept in their place are quite familiar with regular institutionalized mass outbursts of free sex, such as carnivals. In fact, since sex is the cheapest form of enjoyment as well as the most intense (as the Neapolitans say, bed is the poor man's grand opera), it is politically very advantageous, other things being equal, to get them to practice it as much as possible.

In other words, there is no necessary connection between social or political censorship and moral censorship, though it is often assumed that there is. To transfer some kinds of statement of behavior from the impermissible to the publicly permitted is a political act only if it implies changing political relations. Winning the right for white and black to make love in South Africa would be a political act, not because it widens the range of what is sexually allowed but because it attacks racial subjection. Winning the right to publish *Lady Chatterley* has no such implications, though it may be welcomed on other grounds.

This should be abundantly clear from our own experience. Within the last few years the official or conventional prohibitions on what can be said, heard, done, and shown about sex in public—or for that matter in private—have been virtually abolished in several western countries. The belief that a narrow sexual morality is an essential bulwark of the capitalist system is no longer tenable. Nor, indeed, is the belief that the fight against such a morality is very urgent. There are still a few outdated crusaders who may think of themselves as storming a puritan fortress, but in fact its walls have been virtually razed.

No doubt there are still things that cannot be printed or shown but they are progressively harder to find and to get indignant about. The abolition of censorship is a one-dimensional activity, like the movement of women's necklines and skirts, and if that movement goes on too long in a single direction, the returns in revolutionary satisfaction of the crusaders diminish sharply. The right of actors to fuck each other on stage is palpably a less important advance even of personal liberation than the right of Victorian girls to ride bicycles was. It is today becoming quite hard even to mobilize those prosecutions of obscenity on which publishers and producers have so long relied for free publicity.

For practical purposes the battle for public sex has been won. Has this brought social revolution any nearer, or indeed any change outside the bed, the printed page, and public entertainment (which may or may not be desirable)? There is no sign of it. All it has obviously brought is a lot more public sex in an otherwise unchanged social order.

But if there is no intrinsic connection between sexual permissiveness and social organization, there *is*, I am bound to note with a little regret, a persistent affinity between revolution and puritanism. I can think of no well-established organized revolutionary movement or regime which has not developed marked puritanical tendencies. Including marxist ones, whose founders' doctrine was quite unpuritanical (or in Engels's case actively anti-puritanical). Including those in countries like Cuba, whose native tradition is the opposite of puritan. Including the most officially anarchist-libertarian ones. Anyone who believes that the morality of the old anarchist militants was free and easy, does not know what he or she is talking about. Free love (in which they believed passionately) meant no drink, no drugs and monogamy without a formal marriage.

The libertarian, or more exactly antinomian, component of revolutionary movements, though sometimes strong and even dominant at the actual moment of liberation, has never been able to resist the puritan. The Robespierres always win out over the Dantons. Those revolutionaries for whom sexual, or for that matter cultural, libertarianism are really central issues of the revolution are sooner or later edged aside by it. Wilhelm Reich, the apostle of the orgasm, did indeed start out, as the New Left reminds us, as a revolutionary marxist-cum-freudian and a very able one, to judge by his *Mass Psychology of Fascism* (which was subtitled *The sexual economy of political reaction and proletarian sexual policy*). But can we be really surprised that such a man ended by concentrating his interest on orgasm rather than organization? Neither stalinists nor trotskyites felt any enthusiasm for the revolutionary surrealists who hammered at their gates asking to be admitted. Those who survived in politics did not do so as surrealists.

Why this is so is an important and obscure question, which cannot be answered here. Whether it is necessarily so is an even more important question—at all events for revolutionaries who think the official puritanism of revolutionary regimes excessive and often beside the point. But that the great revolutions of our century have not been devoted to sexual permissiveness can hardly be denied. They have advanced sexual freedom (and fundamentally) not by abolishing *sexual* prohibitions, but by a major act of *social* emancipation: the liberation of women from their oppression. And that revolutionary movements have found personal libertarianism a nuisance is also beyond question. One of the big issues today in SDS (Students for a Democratic Society) is whether militants should take drugs.

The whole business is really part of a much wider question. What is the role in revolution or any social change of that cultural rebellion which is today so visible a part of the left, and in certain countries such as the United States the predominant aspect of it? There is no great social revolution which is not combined, at least peripherally, with such cultural dissidence. Perhaps today in the west, where "alienation" rather than poverty is the crucial motive-force of rebellion, no movement which does not also attack the system of personal relations and private satisfactions can be revolutionary. But taken by themselves, cultural revolt and cultural dissidence are symptoms, not revolutionary forces and not very important.

The Russian Revolution of 1917 reduced Dada to its proper social and political proportions. When the French went on general strike in May 1968, the happenings in the Odeon Theatre and that splendid graffiti ("It is forbidden to forbid," "When I make revolution it makes me feel like making love") could be seen to be forms of minor literature and theater, marginal to the main events. The more prominent Dada and similar phenomena are, the more confident we can be that the big things are not happening. Shocking the bourgeois is, alas, easier than overthrowing him.

## *Ernest Becker*

---

# *EVERYMAN AS PERVERT*

If fetishism, by definition, connotes the merger of poverty and ingenuity, we also know that none of us is exempt from the "disease." We are all relatively poor and ingenious. This is what permits us to handle, with full devotion and finely tuned capability, a very definite area of the object world. Without routine compulsiveness, we would all literally fade away; we would be able to marshal no ego at all. The more our powers are limited, and the more some special commitment is wanted, the more we become alert to fetishistic cues to action. They give us a quick definition, an easy commitment, a rapid summing-up of *just what powers and how much care* we need to bring to bear in a particular situation. Thus we are all more or less prone to fetishistic definitions in our sex life when we show a preference for a particular portion of our partner's body. There is nothing about a large breast per se that has any more inherent sexual stimulation to the partner than a small one. Obviously it is all in the eye of the beholder. But our culture teaches us to become committed in *some*

---

*Editor's note:* Becker arrives at this definition with the aid of Simon Nagler who writes that the fetishist is "an insecure, passive, dependent, and inadequate male, whose auto-erotic and diminished sexual activity is simply a reflection of general inactivity." To Simon's notion of psychic emptiness, Becker adds the fetishist's need to create a rich object world in order to invest his life with meaning. See Becker's *Angel in Armor* (New York: George Braziller, 1969), 13, 14.

way to the body of the opposite sex, and we are eager for cues which give us a passport to permissive excitation. When we learn such a cue, we invest it with rich significance. Each culture heightens the meaning of certain qualities of objects so that its members can easily bring into play the approved responsive behavior: lace underwear and steatopygia for sex objects, tailfins and chrome for cars. The easy mark of "beauty" that serves as a perceptual counter is a promise that socially approved satisfaction will be forthcoming. The identifying body part signals, in encapsulated form, an entire range of meanings—of cause-and-effect sequences to be expected. It is as though the individual says: "By focusing my attention on this, I can safely proceed to derive sexual satisfaction and fulfill the proper sex role."

One can easily see that in a very real sense, almost all of man's cultural life takes place on a fetishistic level. Philosophers have taught us that we can never know objects in all their potential fullness. As Diderot, Comte, Whitehead, and others understood, our nervous system itself is *already* a limitation, a sentence to a distorted and partial object world. We can respond to an object largely only in terms of what we *can do* to it, and in this we are limited by the inheritance of millions of years of adaptive evolution. By the very nature of our immersion in a limitless universe, while possessing only limited capacities, we are condemned to a "normal" fetishism. Our world has already been delivered to us abstracted. The mission of both science and art, as the highest human strivings, is to create new objects and to reveal facets of old objects that we did not know existed. The lower animals, after all, are fetishists *par excellence:* they are securely built into a limited range of responsiveness to the merest fragments of objects—an odor, a colored stripe, a hiss. It is given to man alone to break out, somewhat, of the fetishistic world to which nature has condemned sense creatures.

The inanimate fetish object, then, is merely a further symbolic reduction of the fetishistic body part. For the extreme fetishist, it seems that even the organic body part itself, say, a breast, calls out a range of behavior that is too demanding or too threatening. It has been often noted that masturbation is nearly the sole sexual activity of the true fetishist, and this is what we would expect. When one relates to the object as a part object, whether it is an outsized breast or an inanimate object like a shoe, one is *essentially* masturbating. To the extent that one does not need "permission" to be sexual, or does not need a special body contour or identifiable object to trigger this behavior —to that extent one can relate to (more of) the totality of the other person, the sex partner. But, theoretically at any rate, *some* "masturbation" is implicit in using the body of the opposite sex for *some* clues—that is, *in having to identify the partner as a sex object at all.* That is to say, the very identification of the partner as a sex object invites a degree of inversion that we could consider masturbatory. Logically, this is unavoidable: if we were to relate to the object as a total object, *it would cease to be a sexual object at all.* Thus, in "normal" sexual behavior, we try to gain some approximation of a total relationship to the object, even while using an avenue of approach that inevitably reduces it initially to a part-object status.

The fetishist, then, as someone who is severely limited in his behavior, is not—as we stressed above—deprived of resourcefulness. On the contrary, being limited in behavior, he is tasked to create *an extra charge of life-enhancing meaning in a more limited area* than that necessary for the rest of us. That is to say, he must fix on some perceptual detail, and derive the *full justification for drawing himself to the object* from this very narrow focalization. It is this very resourcefulness that appears to the outsider as "abnormal." Let us try to imagine some of what is going on in the extreme fetishist's world. When he says "Your boots are driving me crazy!" he is simply extending or varying the common remark: "Your breasts are driving me crazy!" The fetishist is being drawn perceptually (behaviorally) into the object world by this focal detail. Hence, the tantalizing, frustrating nature of the fetish object to the fetishist's craving. It is a *supercharged* locus of meaning, self-designated as of supreme importance for potential satisfaction. Obviously, the fetish object itself cannot conceivably fulfill the promise of satisfaction with which it has been burdened: hence, the fetishist is caught in a maddening bind. Of course, the object is driving him crazy. He is forced to overinvest in the promise of the largely symbolic fetish object due to his own behavioral poverty; while, at the same time, this symbolic overinvestment cannot be actively repaid by transacting with the simple part object itself. A breast or a shoe simply cannot, by their nature, reward the promise the fetishist has read into them. (How many youths have not been astonished and let down by their first full view of the long-coveted female breast: it seems so oddly without character, for an object that had been invested with so much promise. Compared to the woman's face, this blank expanse of flesh is almost insultingly poor.)

After all, the fetishist is not doing anything more than the street corner ogler of girls who whistles low and agitatedly shouts "Look at that!" By means of unique, exciting, and pleasure-promising objects we draw ourselves into the world, and it becomes alive. Our potential separation is overcome, we are recommitted to the life process, substantiated in the world by means of electric contact with another *real* object. We use the object, as we noted above, to draw ourselves directly into the world. Without objects to commit our attention and striving we do not exist. Experiments on sensory deprivation are interesting mainly in that they prove our plight, our utter dependence on the object world for the coming into being of our directive powers.

And so the fatal passivity of the fetishist. When we elaborate on a part object in order to draw ourselves into the world we are actually affirming our behavioral poverty. The fetishist is condemned to passivity, and reinforces his sentence. Since there is little that one *can do* to a part object because it represents the willful reduction of a situation that invites a fuller range of action, the fetishist is *necessarily passive.* The focal relationship to the part object, that is, blots out other whole areas of possible relationship, and one can muster only a part action. The masturbatory act is all that remains reasonably to be done in the face of a shoe or a corset.

The question that arises in all part-object relationships is this: How far can one narrow down his grip on the world, and *still be in it* in "human" fashion? The fetishist is said to be near to psychosis precisely because his wedge into the object world is so narrow. In extreme schizophrenia we see such a ludicrous narrowing down of the schizophrenic's hold on the world: he seems to be making last-ditch efforts to relate to whatever objects his powers can muster a response to—bits of debris to stuff into body crevices—ultimately his own excrement, anything tangible with which to come into safe manipulatory contact. This represents a degradation of his executive powers to the near-zero level, rather than any peculiarly "mental" aberration.

*Thomas Nagel*

# *SEXUAL PERVERSION*

There is something to be learned about sex from the fact that we possess a concept of sexual perversion. I wish to examine the concept, defending it against the charge of unintelligibility and trying to say exactly what about human sexuality qualifies it to admit of perversions. Let me make some preliminary comments about the problem before embarking on its solution.

Some people do not believe that the notion of sexual perversion makes sense, and even those who do disagree over its application. Nevertheless I think it will be widely conceded that, if the concept is viable at all, it must meet certain general conditions. First, if there are any sexual perversions, they will have to be sexual desires or practices that can be plausibly described as in some sense unnatural, though the explanation of this natural/unnatural distinction is of course the main problem. Second, certain practices will be perversions if anything is, such as shoe fetishism, bestiality, and sadism; other practices, such as unadorned sexual intercourse, will not be; about still others there is controversy. Third, if there are perversions, they will be unnatural sexual *inclinations* rather than merely unnatural practices adopted not from inclination but for other reasons. I realize that this is at variance with the view, maintained by some Roman Catholics, that contraception is a sexual perversion. But although contraception may qualify as a deliberate perversion of the sexual and reproductive functions, it cannot be significantly described as a *sexual* perversion. A sexual perversion must reveal itself in conduct that expresses an unnatural *sexual* preference. And although there might be a form of fetishism focused on the employment of contraceptive devices, that is not the usual explanation for their use.

I wish to declare at the outset my belief that the connection between sex and reproduction has no bearing on sexual perversion. The latter is a concept of psychological, not physiological interest, and it is a concept that we do not apply to the lower animals, let alone to plants, all of which have reproductive functions that can go astray in various ways. (Think of seedless oranges.) Insofar as we are prepared to regard higher animals as perverted, it is because of their psychological rather than their anatomical similarity to humans. Furthermore, we do not regard as a perversion every deviation from the reproductive function of sex in humans: sterility, miscarriage, contraception, abortion.

Another matter that I believe has no bearing on the concept of sexual perversion is social disapprobation or custom. Anyone inclined to think that in each society the perversions are those sexual practices of which the community disapproves should consider all the societies that have frowned upon adultery and fornication. These have not been regarded as unnatural practices, but have been thought objectionable in other ways. What is regarded as unnatural admittedly varies from culture to culture, but the classification is not a pure expression of disapproval or distaste. In fact it is often regarded as a *ground* for disapproval, and that suggests that the classification has an independent content.

I am going to attempt a psychological account of sexual perversion, which will depend on a specific psychological theory of sexual desire and human sexual interactions. To approach this solution I wish first to consider a contrary position, one which provides a basis for skepticism about the existence of any sexual perversions at all, and perhaps about the very significance of the term. The skeptical argument runs as follows:

> Sexual desire is simply one of the appetities, like hunger and thirst. As such it may have various objects, some more common than others perhaps, but none in any sense 'natural.' An appetite is identified as sexual by means of the organs and erogenous zones in which its satisfaction can be to some extent localized, and the special sensory pleasures which form the core of that satisfaction. This enables us to recognize widely divergent goals, activities, and desires as sexual, since it is conceivable in principle that anything should produce sexual pleasure and that a nondeliberate, sexually charged desire for it should arise (as a result of conditioning, if nothing else). We may fail to empathize with some of these desires, and some of them, like sadism, may be objectionable on extraneous grounds, but once we have observed that they meet the criteria for being sexual, there is nothing more to be said on *that* score. Either they are sexual or they are not; sexuality does not admit of imperfection, or perversion, or any other such qualification—it is not that sort of affection.

This is probably the received radical position. It suggests that the cost of defending a psychological account may be to deny that sexual desire is an appetite. But insofar as that line of defense is plausible, it should make us suspicious of the simple picture of appetites on which the skepticism depends. Perhaps the standard appetites, like hunger, cannot be classed as pure appetites in that sense either, at least in their human versions.

Let us approach the matter by asking whether we can imagine anything that would qualify as a gastronomical perversion. Hunger and eating are importantly like sex in that they serve a biological function and also play a significant role in our inner lives. It is noteworthy that there is little temptation to describe as perverted an appetite for substances that are not nourishing. We should probably not consider someone's appetites as *perverted* if he liked to eat paper, sand, wood, or cotton. Those are merely rather odd and very unhealthy tastes: they lack the psychological complexity that we expect of perversions. (Coprophilia, being already a sexual perversion, may be disregarded.) If on the other hand someone liked to eat cookbooks, or magazines with pictures of food in them, and preferred these to ordinary food—or if when hungry he sought satisfaction by fondling a napkin or ashtray from his favorite restaurant—then the concept of perversion might seem appropriate (in fact it would be natural to describe this as a case of gastronomical fetishism). It would be natural to describe as gastronomically perverted someone who could eat only by having food forced down his throat through a funnel, or only if the meal were a living animal. What helps in such cases is the peculiarity of the desire itself, rather than the inappropriateness of its object to the biological function that the desire serves. Even an appetite, it would seem, can have perversions if in addition to its biological function it has a significant psychological structure.

In the case of hunger, psychological complexity is provided by the activities that give it expression. Hunger is not merely a disturbing sensation that can be quelled by eating; it is an attitude toward edible portions of the external world, a desire to relate to them in rather special ways. The method of ingestion: chewing, savoring, swallowing, appreciating the texture and smell, all are important components of the relation, as is the passivity and controllability of the food (the only animals we eat live are helpless mollusks). Our relation to food depends also on our size: we do not live upon it or burrow into it like aphids or worms. Some of these features are more central than others, but any adequate phenomenology of eating would have to treat it as a relation to the external world and a way of appropriating bits of that world, with characteristic affection. Displacements or serious restrictions of the desire to eat could then be described as perversions, if they undermined that direct relation between man and food which is the natural expression of hunger. This explains why it is easy to imagine gastronomical fetishism, voyeurism, exhibitionism, or even gastronomical sadism and masochism. Indeed some of these perversions are fairly common.

If we can imagine perversions of an appetite like hunger, it should be possible to make sense of the concept of sexual perversion. I do not wish to imply that sexual desire is an appetite—only that being an appetite is no bar to admitting of perversions. Like hunger, sexual desire has as its characteristic object a certain relation with something in the external world; only in this case it is usually a person rather than an omelet, and the relation is considerably more complicated. This added complication allows scope for correspondingly complicated perversions.

The fact that sexual desire is a feeling about other persons may tempt us to take a pious view of its psychological content. There are those who believe that sexual desire is properly the expression of some other attitude, like love, and that when it occurs by itself it is incomplete and unhealthy—or at any rate subhuman. (The extreme Platonic version of such a view is that sexual practices are all vain attempts to express something they cannot in principle achieve: this makes them all perversions, in a sense.) I do not believe that any such view is correct. Sexual desire is complicated enough without having to be linked to anything else as a condition for phenomenological analysis. It cannot be denied that sex may serve various functions—economic, social, altruistic—but it also has its own content as a relation between persons, and it is only by analyzing that relation that we can understand the conditions of sexual perversion.

I believe it is very important that the object of sexual attraction is a particular individual, who transcends the properties that make him attractive. When different persons are attracted to a single person for different reasons—eyes, hair, figure, laugh, intelligence—we feel that the object of their desire is nevertheless the same, namely that person. There is even an inclination to feel that this is so if the lovers have different sexual aims, if they include both men and women, for example. Different specific attractive characteristics seem to provide enabling conditions for the operation of a single basic feeling, and the different aims all provide expressions of it. We approach the sexual attitude toward the person through the features that we find attractive, but these features are not the objects of that attitude.

This is very different from the case of an omelet. Various people may desire it for different reasons—one for its fluffiness, another for its mushrooms, another for its unique combination of aroma and visual aspect; yet we do not enshrine the transcendental omelet as the true common object of their affections. Instead we might say that several desires have accidentally converged on the same object: any omelet with the crucial characteristics would do as well. It is not similarly true that any person with the same flesh distribution and way of smoking can be substituted as object for a particular sexual desire that has been elicited by those characteristics. It may be that they will arouse attraction whenever they recur, but it will be a new sexual attraction with a new particular object, not merely a transfer of the old desire to someone else. (I believe this is true even in cases where the new object is unconsciously identified with a former one.)

The importance of this point will emerge when we see how complex a psychological interchange constitutes the natural development of sexual attraction. This would be incomprehensible if its object were not a particular person, but rather a person of a certain *kind*. Attraction is only the beginning, and fulfillment does not consist merely of behavior and contact expressing this attraction, but involves much more.

The best discussion of these matters that I have seen appears in part III of Sartre's *Being and Nothingness*.[1] Since it has influenced my own views, I shall say a few things about it now. Sartre's treatment of sexual desire and of love, hate, sadism, masochism, and further attitudes toward others depends on a general theory of consciousness and the body which we can neither expound nor assume here. He does not discuss perversion, and this is partly because he regards sexual desire as one form of the perpetual attempt of an embodied consciousness to come to terms with the existence of others, an attempt that is as doomed to fail in this form as it is in any of the others, which include sadism and masochism (if not certain of the more impersonal deviations) as well as several nonsexual attitudes. According to Sartre, all attempts to incorporate the other into my world as another subject, i.e., to apprehend him at once as an object for me and as a subject for whom I am an object, are unstable and doomed to collapse into one or other of the two aspects. Either I reduce him entirely to an object, in which case his subjectivity escapes the possession or appropriation I can extend to that object; or I become merely an object for him, in which case I am no longer in a position to appropriate his subjectivity. Moreover, neither of these aspects is stable; each is continually in danger of giving way to the other. This has the consequence that there can be no such thing as a *success-*

---

[1] Translated by Hazel E. Barnes (New York: Philosophical Library: 1956).

*ful* sexual relation, since the deep aim of sexual desire cannot in principle be accomplished. It seems likely, therefore, that the view will not permit a basic distinction between successful or complete and unsuccessful or incomplete sex, and therefore cannot admit the concept of perversion.

I do not adopt this aspect of the theory, nor many of its metaphysical underpinnings. What interests me is Sartre's picture of the attempt. He says that the type of possession that is the object of sexual desire is carried out by "a double reciprocal incarnation" and that this is accomplished, typically in the form of a caress, in the following way: "I make myself flesh in order to impel the Other to realize *for herself* and *for me* her own flesh, and my caresses cause my flesh to be born for me in so far as it is for the Other *flesh causing her to be born as flesh*" (p. 391, italics Sartre's). The incarnation in question is described variously as a clogging or troubling of consciousness, which is inundated by the flesh in which it is embodied.

The view I am going to suggest, I hope in less obscure language, is related to this one, but it differs from Sartre's in allowing sexuality to achieve its goal on occasion and thus in providing the concept of perversion with a foothold.

Sexual desire involves a kind of perception, but not merely a single perception of its object, for in the paradigm case of mutual desire there is a complex system of superimposed mutual perceptions—not only perceptions of the sexual object, but perceptions of oneself. Moreover, sexual awareness of another involves considerable self-awareness to begin with—more than is involved in ordinary sensory perception. The experience is felt as an assault on oneself by the view (or touch, or whatever) of the sexual object.

Let us consider a case in which the elements can be separated. For clarity we will restrict ourselves initially to the somewhat artificial case of desire at a distance. Suppose a man and a woman, whom we may call Romeo and Juliet, are at opposite ends of a cocktail lounge, with many mirrors on the walls which permit unobserved observation, and even mutual unobserved observation. Each of them is sipping a martini and studying other people in the mirrors. At some point Romeo notices Juliet. He is moved, somehow, by the softness of her hair and the diffidence with which she sips her martini, and this arouses him sexually. Let us say that *X senses Y* whenever *X* regards *Y* with sexual desire. (*Y* need not be a person, and *X*'s apprehension of *Y* can be visual, tactile, olfactory, etc., or purely imaginary; in the present example we shall concentrate on vision.) So Romeo senses Juliet, rather than merely noticing her. At this stage he is aroused by an unaroused object, so he is more in the sexual grip of his body than she of hers.

Let us suppose, however, that Juliet now senses Romeo in another mirror on the opposite wall, though neither of them yet knows that he is seen by the other (the mirror angles provide three-quarter views). Romeo then begins to notice in Juliet the subtle signs of sexual arousal: heavy-lidded stare, dilating pupils, faint flush, et cetera. This of course renders her much more bodily, and he not only notices but senses this as well. His arousal is nevertheless still solitary. But now, cleverly calculating the line of her stare without actually looking her in the eyes, he realizes that it is directed at him through the mirror on the opposite wall. That is, he notices, and moreover senses, Juliet sensing him. This is definitely a new development, for it gives him a sense of embodiment not only through his own reactions but through the eyes and reactions of another. Moreover, it is separable from the initial sensing of Juliet; for sexual arousal might begin with a person's sensing that he is sensed and being assailed by the perception of the other person's desire rather than merely by the perception of the person.

But there is a further step. Let us suppose that Juliet, who is a little slower than Romeo, now senses that he senses her. This puts Romeo in a position to notice, and be aroused by, her arousal at being sensed by him. He senses that she senses that he senses her. This is still another level of arousal, for he becomes conscious of his sexuality through his awareness of its effect on her and of her awareness that this effect is due to him. Once she takes the same step and senses that he senses her sensing him, it becomes difficult to state, let alone imagine, further iterations, though they may be logically distinct. If both are alone, they will presumably turn to look at each other directly, and the proceedings will continue on another plane. Physical contact and intercourse are perfectly natural extensions of this complicated visual exchange, and mutual touch can involve all the complexities of awareness present in the visual case, but with a far greater range of subtlety and acuteness.

Ordinarily, of course, things happen in a less orderly fashion—sometimes in a great rush—but I believe that some version of this overlapping system of distinct sexual perceptions and interactions is the basic framework of any full-fledged sexual relation and that relations involving only part of the complex are significantly incomplete. The account is only schematic, as it must be to achieve generality. Every real sexual act will be psychologically far more specific and detailed, in ways that depend not only on the physical techniques employed and on anatomical details, but also on countless features of the participants' conceptions of themselves and of each other, which become embodied in the act. (It is a familiar enough fact, for example, that people often take their social roles and the social roles of their partners to bed with them.)

The general schema is important, however, and the proliferation of levels of mutual awareness it involves is an example of a type of complexity that typifies human interactions. Consider aggression, for example. If I am angry with someone, I want to make him feel it, either to produce self-reproach by getting him to see himself through the eyes of my anger, and to dislike what he sees—or else to produce reciprocal anger or fear, by getting him to perceive my anger as a threat or attack. What I want will depend on the details of my anger, but in either case it will involve a desire that the object of that anger be aroused. This accomplishment constitutes the fulfillment of my emotion, through domination of the object's feelings.

Another example of such reflexive mutual recognition is to be found in the phenomenon of meaning, which appears to involve an intention to produce a belief or other effect in another by bringing about his recognition of one's intention to produce that effect. Sex has a related structure: it involves a desire that one's partner be aroused by the recognition of one's desire that he or she be aroused.

It is not easy to define the basic types of awareness and arousal of which these complexes are composed, and that remains a lacuna in this discussion. I believe that the object of awareness is the same in one's own case as it is in one's sexual awareness of another, although the two awarenesses will not be the same, the difference being as great as that between feeling angry and experiencing the anger of another. All stages of sexual perception are varieties of identification of a person with his body. What is perceived is one's own or another's *subjection* to or *immersion* in his body, a phenomenon which has been recognized with loathing by St. Paul and St. Augustine, both of whom regarded "the law of sin which is in my members" as a grave threat to the dominion of the holy will.[2] In sex-

---

[2] See Romans, VII, 23; and the *Confessions*, Book 8, v.

ual desire and its expression the blending of involuntary response with deliberate control is extremely important. For Augustine, the revolution launched against him by his body is symbolized by erection and the other involuntary physical components of arousal. Sartre too stresses the fact that the penis is not a prehensile organ. But mere involuntariness characterizes other bodily processes as well. In sexual desire the involuntary responses are combined with submission to spontaneous impulses: not only one's pulse and secretions but one's actions are taken over by the body; ideally, deliberate control is needed only to guide the expression of those impulses. This is to some extent also true of an appetite like hunger, but the takeover there is more localized, less pervasive, less extreme. One's whole body does not become saturated with hunger as it can with desire. But the most characteristic feature of a specifically sexual immersion in the body is its ability to fit into the complex of mutual perceptions that we have described. Hunger leads to spontaneous interactions with food; sexual desire leads to spontaneous interactions with other persons, whose bodies are asserting their sovereignty in the same way, producing involuntary reactions and spontaneous impulses in *them*. These reactions are perceived, and the perception of them is perceived, and that perception is in turn perceived; at each step the domination of the person by his body is reinforced, and the sexual partner becomes more possessible by physical contact, penetration, and envelopment.

Desire is therefore not merely the perception of a preexisting embodiment of the other, but ideally a contribution to his further embodiment which in turn enhances the original subject's sense of himself. This explains why it is important that the partner be aroused, and not merely aroused, but aroused by the awareness of one's desire. It also explains the sense in which desire has unity and possession as its object: physical possession must eventuate in creation of the sexual object in the image of one's desire, and not merely in the object's recognition of that desire, or in his or her own private arousal.

To return, finally, to the topic of perversion: I believe that various familiar deviations constitute truncated or incomplete versions of the complete configuration, and may therefore be regarded as perversions of the central impulse.

In particular, narcissistic practices and intercourse with animals, infants, and inanimate objects seem to be stuck at some primitive version of the first stage. If the object is not alive, the experience is reduced entirely to an awareness of one's own sexual embodiment. Small children and animals permit awareness of the embodiment of the other, but present obstacles to reciprocity, to the recognition by the sexual object of the subject's desire as the source of his (the object's) sexual self-awareness.

Sadism concentrates on the evocation of passive self-awareness in others, but the sadist's engagement is itself active and requires a retention of deliberate control which impedes awareness of himself as a bodily subject of passion in the required sense. The victim must recognize him as the source of his own sexual passivity, but only as the active source. De Sade claimed that the object of sexual desire was to evoke involuntary responses from one's partner, especially audible ones. The infliction of pain is no doubt the most efficient way to accomplish this, but it requires a certain abrogation of one's own exposed spontaneity. All this, incidentally, helps to explain why it is tempting to regard as sadistic an excessive preoccupation with sexual technique, which does not permit one to abandon the role of agent at any stage of the sexual act. Ideally one should be able to surmount one's technique at some point.

A masochist on the other hand imposes the same disability on his partner as the sadist imposes on himself. The masochist cannot find a satisfactory embodiment as the object of another's sexual desire, but only as the object of his control. He is passive not in relation to his partner's passion but in relation to his nonpassive agency. In addition, the subjection to one's body characteristic of pain and physical restraint is of a very different kind from that of sexual excitement: pain causes people to contract rather than dissolve.

Both of these disorders have to do with the second stage, which involves the awareness of oneself as an object of desire. In straightforward sadism and masochism other attentions are substituted for desire as a source of the object's self-awareness. But it is also possible for nothing of that sort to be substituted, as in the case of a masochist who is satisfied with self-inflicted pain or of a sadist who does not insist on playing a role in the suffering that arouses him. Greater difficulties of classification are presented by three other categories of sexual activity: elaborations of the sexual act; intercourse of more than two persons; and homosexuality.

If we apply our model to the various forms that may be taken by two-party heterosexual intercourse, none of them seems clearly to qualify as perversion. Hardly anyone can be found these days to inveigh against oral-genital contact, and the merits of buggery are urged by such respectable figures as D. H. Lawrence and Norman Mailer. There may be something vaguely sadistic about the latter technique (in Mailer's writings it seems to be a method of introducing an element of rape), but it is not obvious that this has to be so. In general, it would appear that any bodily contact between a man and a woman that gives them sexual pleasure is a possible vehicle for the system of multi-level interpersonal awareness that I have claimed is the basic psychological content of sexual interaction. Thus a liberal platitude about sex is upheld.

About multiple combinations, the least that can be said is that they are bound to be complicated. If one considers how difficult it is to carry on two conversations simultaneously, one may appreciate the problems of multiple simultaneous interpersonal perception that can arise in even a small-scale orgy. It may be inevitable that some of the component relations should degenerate into mutual epidermal stimulation by participants otherwise isolated from each other. There may also be a tendency toward voyeurism and exhibitionism, both of which are incomplete relations. The exhibitionist wishes to display his desire without needing to be desired in return; he may even fear the sexual attentions of others. A voyeur, on the other hand, need not require any recognition by his object at all: certainly not a recognition of the voyeur's arousal.

It is not clear whether homosexuality is a perversion that is measured by the standard of the described configuration, but it seems unlikely. For such a classification would have to depend on the possibility of extracting from the system a distinction between male and female sexuality; and much that has been said so far applies equally to men and women. Moreover, it would have to be maintained that there was a natural tie between the type of sexuality and the sex of the body, and also that two sexualities of the same type could not interact properly.

Certainly there is much support for an aggressive-passive distinction between male and female sexuality. In our culture the male's arousal tends to initiate the perceptual exchange, he usually makes the sexual approach, largely controls the course of the act, and of course penetrates whereas the woman receives. When two men or two women engage in intercourse they cannot both adhere to these sexual roles. The question is how essential the roles are to an adequate sexual relation. One relevant observation is that a good deal of deviation from these roles occurs in heterosexual intercourse. Women can be sexually aggressive and men passive, and temporary reversals of role are not uncommon in heterosexual exchanges of reasonable length. If such conditions are set aside, it may be urged that there is something irreducibly perverted in attraction to a body anatomically like one's own. But alarming as some people in our culture may find such attraction, it remains psychologically unilluminating to class it as perverted. Certainly if homosexuality is a perversion, it is so in a very different sense from that in which shoe fetishism is a perversion, for some version of the full range of interpersonal perceptions seems perfectly possible between two persons of the same sex.

In any case, even if the proposed model is correct, it remains implausible to describe as perverted every deviation from it. For example, if the partners in heterosexual intercourse indulge in private heterosexual fantasies, that obscures the recognition of the real partner and so, on the theory, constitutes a defective sexual relation. It is not, however, generally regarded as a perversion. Such examples suggest that a simple dichotomy between perverted and unperverted sex is too crude to organize the phenomena adequately.

I should like to close with some remarks about the relation of perversion to good, bad, and morality. The concept of perversion can hardly fail to be evaluative in some sense, for it appears to involve the notion of an ideal or at least adequate sexuality which the perversions in some way fail to achieve. So, if the concept is viable, the judgment that a person or practice or desire is perverted will constitute a sexual evaluation, implying that better sex, or a better specimen of sex, is possible. This in itself is a very weak claim, since the evaluation might be in a dimension that is of little interest to us. (Though, if my account is correct, that will not be true.)

Whether it is a moral evaluation, however, is another

question entirely—one whose answer would require more understanding of both morality and perversion than can be deployed here. Moral evaluation of acts and of persons is a rather special and very complicated matter, and by no means are all our evaluations of persons and their activities moral evaluations. We make judgments about people's beauty or health or intelligence which are evaluative without being moral. Assessments of their sexuality may be similar in that respect.

Furthermore, moral issues aside, it is not clear that unperverted sex is necessarily *preferable* to the perversions. It may be that sex which receives the highest marks for perfection *as sex* is less enjoyable than certain perversions; and if enjoyment is considered very important, that might outweigh considerations of sexual perfection in determining rational preference.

That raises the question of the relation between the evaluative content of judgments of perversion and the rather common *general* distinction between good and bad sex. The latter distinction is usually confined to sexual acts, and it would seem, within limits, to cut across the other: even someone who believed, for example, that homosexuality was a perversion could admit a distinction between better and worse homosexual sex, and might even allow that good homosexual sex could be better *sex* than not very good unperverted sex. If this is correct, it supports the position that, if judgments of perversion are viable at all, they represent only one aspect of the possible evaluation of sex, even *qua sex.* Moreover it is not the only important aspect: certainly sexual deficiencies that evidently do not constitute perversions can be the object of great concern.

Finally, even if perverted sex is to that extent not so good as it might be, bad sex is generally better than none at all. This should not be controversial: it seems to hold for other important matters, like food, music, literature, and society. In the end, one must choose from among the available alternatives, whether their availability depends on the environment or on one's own constitution. And the alternatives have to be fairly grim before it becomes rational to opt for nothing.

## *Dorothy Kalins*

---

# *VOYEURISM IN NEW YORK*

In an apartment building on the East Side, a girl stands in her living room, ironing. The shades are up, and she has no clothes on. Two blocks away, in a similar building directly facing hers, a man is looking through a telescope. He has been watching her for a long time. He knows what her boyfriend looks like. He knows her expression as the boyfriend approaches while she irons. . . . His telescope is permanently mounted on a bookcase, and friends regard it as a piece of sculpture.

In another East Side building, this time further uptown, a young man goes up to his roof at a special time each night. He sweeps his telescope over the four sides of the buildings facing his. He focuses on special windows. Once in a while he whistles a signal to his friends. They are on top of the adjacent buildings, looking back.

On West 76th Street a couple has just gone into a shower together. The man across the street is tense and anxious. Is the steam from the bathroom going to come out and fog up the windows before they do?

A brilliant young investment banker takes you out to the back terrace of his Sixties brownstone. He's not trying to mess around. What he wants to show you is how with his tiny monocular telescope he can check out a whole open-ended back yard of windows. He tells you his main looking principles: "You've got to wait till they get to the kitchen—that's where the light is best," and "It is much better to concentrate on a little flabbiness close by than the promise of something better too far away to see." Back inside, you don't have to explain to his wife where you've been. She was the one instructed to find an apartment with a backyard terrace in the first place.

Voyeurism, in the classical sense, is a perversion where the sexual gratification of looking replaces the gratification of doing. Freudians call it by ominous, guilt-ridden names like *mixoscopia* and connect it with castration anxiety: If a person can be sexually satisfied by watching someone else perform a threatening act, he is reassured and released from responsibility. Today, however, psychological opinion holds that voyeurism (excepting its pathological extremes) is an essentially positive act—a participation with the visual senses that enhances the aesthetics of sex. As long as visual stimulation doesn't replace The Real Thing (modern voyeurs rarely look at The Real Thing, anyway) voyeurism can be a very important element in heightening sexual experience.

Voyeurism is an implicit life process in this city, with its own set of rules and locations. It has suddenly become okay to acknowledge at-home looking habits—at least to friends. There is nothing covert about using binoculars and telescopes. Looking isn't only confined to standard how-can-you-help-but-see views from buildings sliced open like ant farms. It is more frequent and more obvious —on streets, in subways, in lines. The whole mode of voyeurism has been ritualized to intensify the stimulation people get from watching other people—places such as discothèques, shops, certain restaurants, movies, the theater. It has become just as permissible for a public place to exploit voyeuristic tendencies as it is for a person to talk openly about his voyeuristic practices.

People with handy telescopes or binoculars consider themselves Gentleman Lookers. There is titillation but no guilt in the stories they tell. They say things like "Voyeurism is a holiday, life without risk, an escape *into* reality. A game with the senses. A way of creating drama, of charging life with extra excitement. A way to break down city loneliness. Everything out there is a play for your benefit." What they don't say is perhaps more important—that you don't have to *do* anything. If you wonder what Gentleman Lookers spend their time looking at, the answer is obvious: ladies. The next question is harder to answer. Is the vice versa?

The ostensible object of voyeurism is the naked body. There is a traditional division of roles: men are voyeuristic; women, exhibitionistic. Women display more. They use nonverbal cues in an aggressively subtle attempt to evoke a man's response. Obviously, small bathing suits and no underwear are tacit signals: "I am doing this so you'll look at me." After all, if society demands that a woman must be pursued, she has to do something to attract the pursuer.

Traditionally, women are attracted to action, men to form. But these kinds of traditions are not easy to accept, especially by women who refuse to believe that men experience *anything* to a greater degree than they. It is not hard to find good examples of how roles are changing. The clues are in clothing, the function of which has never been to conceal the body but to draw attention to it. Physically revealing male dress used to be purely a homosexual phenomenon, worn with the same exhibitionistic motives women have. But for a long time, men have been spending as much time on Savile Row and at Dunhill as many women at the dressmaker's; even if the result is more English banker than Cardin, the psychology of drawing attention to the body is the same. What *Esquire* calls the Peacock Revolution in men's fashion, a more overtly sexual way of dressing, has come about because society encourages all kinds of self expression.

As men become more exhibitionistic, women become

more stimulated by the things that stimulate men—revealing clothing, and less of it. Last spring when this town's version of Naked Ike walked across Times Square, the most attention he drew was from a beauty parlor full of women, who knocked each other out of the way to get a better look.

Suggesting these evidences of role-reversal, I asked a New York psychiatrist if the exchange would ever be complete. He acknowledged a substantial amount of slippage in the voyeuristic-exhibitionistic balance, but he felt unequivocally that there would never be a man-woman equality of roles.

> The biology of the situation will break it down. Attempts to emphasize male beauty will never serve the same evocative purpose as female beauty. Pretty long hair or a nipped-in waist is usually not enough to turn a woman on. Women depend more on mental distinctions and are receptive to male beauty only after the demands of personal rapport, intimate interchange and the answer to 'What does he think of me?' have been explored. Women usually describe men in the unphysical terms of 'interesting looking.'
>
> On the other hand, a man has to work very hard to develop a profound cerebral response to a woman because his initial physical sense of her—what she looks and smells and feels like—is so emphatic.

Voyeuristic stimulation is an intensely personal thing. What turns someone on visually is a complex combination of his personality and where he chooses to look.

Of all the looking-places in the city, the most intimate is the home. Everywhere else people consciously or unconsciously assume a public behavior. But when you look at people at home, you're seeing *privacy*. To the purist (my source is an English professor friend who psyched it all out long ago) this is the real, most intense voyeuristic experience. Life. It goes with the feeling "We're really getting it. This is what is really happening." There is a quality of breathless suspense: "Are we going to see it?"—whatever *it* might be.

*It* is usually some girl, dressed, undressed or in the process. In any case, the voyeur renounces all responsibility by beginning the stories with "She left the shades up" or "She never pulls the shades down." The reason the shades are up at all is another matter entirely. Maybe she has never admitted that she lives in a city with eight million other people. At any rate, her presence is not necessarily exhibitionistic in the voyeur's mind. The essential thing is that he must believe that if she knew she was being observed, she would immediately pull the shades. She must never know that the concept of privacy has broken down. Once she acknowledges that, he loses his pleasure in watching.

At one time a group of people would gather in a large West Side apartment, sit in the dark and look at a couple cavorting in an apartment across the street. One night some guy came into the "peepage" room and turned on the lights, immediately revealing to the couple that all these people were looking at them. Instead of closing the curtains, the couple started to put on nightly shows, holding sheets in front of their mingling silhouettes. The effect was a cartoon of the real thing, and the group lost all excitement and interest in watching.

The people being observed must remain strangers for another reason—to allow the looker to attach all kinds of personal fantasies and identities to them. One man, all caught up with a couple across the street who can only be seen by the light of the television set, becomes really anxious about their well-being when the TV is off and he can't see what they are doing.

My friend the professor says there is an art of looking that gets you right to the real sense of the life you're watching. The art is a precision and economy of looking: not reacting to false clues; being able to read and understand all kinds of habitual movement so that every looking escapade is rewarded because you can sense when something important is going to happen.

There is a girl across the street from my friend whose living patterns he was beginning to master. One night he saw this girl making getting-ready-for-a-date motions. When she was dressed, he kept watching to see the guy she was waiting for. A long time passed. He sensed her increasing nervousness. She walked around the room, picking up things, putting them down. He suddenly knew that she thought she had been stood up, diagnosed her rejection and waited with her. The guy finally got there and rang the bell. But she wouldn't answer. She sat and didn't move even when he stood in front of the house and yelled her name. He went away. She went to bed. The looker had his perceptions confirmed.

Looking in on people's lives is an agreeable voyeuristic sensation even when there is no intimation of sexuality in what you see. The stimulation is in getting at what used to be withheld. The high-rise, curtain-walled building did more than use glass to impersonate space: it changed our whole concept of privacy. Any two adjacent office buildings on Park Avenue have access to each other's insides. But not much office-to-office looking takes place because the glass becomes more mirror than window and there is painfully little difference between the various desks and cubicles.

When an office building is next to a hotel, as the Grolier Building is to the Summit on Lex, looking is worthwhile. A girl sitting over her midmorning coffee and Danish can be intrigued by some guy in a hotel room pulling on his undershirt.

People used to go to the top of the Beekman for its unparalleled view of the city at night. But now the unparalleled view is of life in UN Plaza, and there is a lot of unclosed curtain wall in those two buildings. A whole set of implicit patterns has reportedly been established in the "lookage" from east to west tower (even though the managing agents keep saying that the buildings are a street's width apart). Apparently, curtains are left open only when something is going on that is chic enough to be seen. One tenant, unable to cope with the proximity of the east tower, built a whole fake-fireplace wall to mask his eastern exposure.

Some people believe that privacy in money machinations is more sacrosanct than privacy in sex. Yet you can walk down any midtown street and see bank vaults in windows open and close for the passers-by. Bank officers are glass housed; for from the sidewalk, any pedestrian can see loans negotiated, men making or breaking other men.

Another curious glass-wall corruption of privacy is the windowed beauty salon. Women who ten years ago used to moan about being seen without their faces on, now quite calmly accept street watchers seeing them without their hair on. (The hair, of course, is on a dummy head being curled and dried next to the real woman and what's left of her real hair.)

On any trip through the ground floor of Bloomingdale's you'll see some woman having a complete make-up job, either oblivous to the public display of her toilette, or basking in it.

"Lookage" on the street is so common and without special titillation that it has become a soda-pop phenomenon. Girl-watching, whether you're standing on the corner or not, is an absent-minded national preoccupation. But a friend from Iowa said this about New York: This city is the only place where when you stare at a girl on the street she is staring right back at you. The same source pointed out his favorite window on Fifth Avenue—a Doubleday bookstore that always attracts a large crowd of men. It turns out that there is a two-story circular staircase, which carries a lot of female traffic, set right in the front window.

A special kind of street watching is that carried on by construction workers, truck drivers, and delivery boys, who keep up a sidewalk badinage when a girl walks by. Even though they break a looker's taboo by talking, the remote quality of the things they say does not reduce the distance between observation and insult. Remarks like "Baby, if I had the afternoon off I'd kidnap you" and "I bless the day I come to this country" are as impersonal as a mute stare, and more interesting. Like the man with the telescope, they don't *do* anything either.

There are certain streets especially charged with voyeuristic appeal. In midtown, 57th Street is what Fifth Avenue used to be before it became too crowded with people in from out of town. Fifty-seventh Street, more specifically the north side between Fifth and Third is the city's great insular stage—a boulevard with enough space to insure anonymity, with enough distance to allow the looking that is understated and, by mutual consent, unspoken. If there is any physical excitement left in seeing a beautiful thing walk closer and closer, hesitate, pass, and walk on, you can find it there.

Street scenes are implicit measuring devices to compare and test all kinds of personal qualities. One obvious scene that works this way is St. Mark's Place, where looking is a life-style. The street is really a modern example of the castration anxiety Freud connected to exhibitionism (as well as voyeurism). The extreme reaction true exhibitionists get when exposing themselves in public reassures them that there is something there to react to in the first place. In the same way, hippie types are reassured by the fascination out-of-townies and straight kids find in them. They need to be watched and reacted to as a constant reminder of their rebellion, assured that they don't look like the suburbs they ran away from.

Last summer a group of hippies filled two Greyhound buses and went to Queens. Their ostensible purpose was to show the people mowing their lawns and sitting on front porches what it felt like to be stared at—the way people from Queens come to stare at them. But the real reason was the release from anxiety. They had to make sure they'd feel out of place off The Place.

Outdoor cafés in New York have never really made it as successful looking-places. The main problem is distance. Sidewalks simply are not wide enough. So the café turns out to be some jerry-built emulation of Le Dôme, awkwardly taking so much space from the sidewalk that pedestrians fall over chairs and railings, somehow removing the voyeuristic mystique that Parisian cafés have so long nurtured.

The only outdoor café that works in this city is the Restaurant in the Park at Bethesda Fountain. Tables are far enough apart (Craig Claiborne's favorite prerequisite) and dining areas line aisles especially geared for prime entrance- and exit-watching.

The quality of distance is vital to voyeuristic experience, particularly in public places. Edward T. Hall's book *The Hidden Dimension* talks about certain distances, measurable in inches, that are required for various levels of intimate, social and business transactions. Hall never came up with an ideal looker's distance, but he did realize that in elevators, for example, it is impossible to do more than stare at passing floor numbers: "In crowded elevators the hands are kept at the sides . . . the eyes are fixed on infinity and not brought to bear on anyone for more than a passing glance." Hall calls this proximity "intimate distance" and calculates the actual space as between six to eighteen inches.

Seeking voyeuristic stimulation on the streets or in the subways is really another way of escaping from the predictability and boredom of routine. In and out of cabs, train stations, subways, the painful and romantic eye-exchange with people you'll never see again is a contrivance to charge the numbing experience of getting from one place to another.

Subways are perfect for playing out personal fantasies on an unsuspecting person across the aisle. You find yourself face-to-face with some deep-eyed type; about the last thing you imagine is what he's really thinking: that his idea of fun is to throw the family into the Volkswagen on Saturday morning and go down to Jensen's for a Danish salad bowl. Or that he's the type whose opinions on things include his wife's. You know: "We thought the book was rather overdone, but then we thought the movie lacked the gut essence of the book."

Public places have always appealed in some degree to voyeuristic impulse. There is a distinction, however, between places that play on sexual looking and those that foster social voyeurism—the to-see-and-be-seen scene. Social voyeurism has as its objective recognition, not titillation. The opera used to be the seat of social voyeurism. Now, however, it takes place mainly in restaurants like Grenouille, Caravelle, Lafayette, etc., where the looks are accompanied by bird-like pecking movements, and facial expressions are curiously out of sync with words. Social voyeurs are characterized by the clothes they like to look at. There is no dress more asexual than *haute couture*. Social lookers lust after power, money, clout—not thighs and legs.

Places that have not been voyeuristically exploited in the past are suddenly the center of much looking activity. Stores, for example, where a lot of dressing and undessing goes on, are prime outposts of the new voyeurism. Alexander's unisex boutique on Eighth Street, called Experiment One, prides itself on a sociologically sophisticated notion of interchangeability of the sexes. So they made boys' clothes look just like girls' clothes. But they also made dressing room doors just wide enough to insure privacy if you're trying on a belt. The clothes may be similar, but the takers off and putters on still aren't, and the numbers of people leaning on counters and racks with affected nonchalance know it. "Do you want any help?" they are asked. "No. We're just looking."

Bert Stern's On First gallery-shop has dressing rooms created with an exhibitionist's fury. Two-way mirrors. They can't see in but you can see out. You're undressing for the crowd. The only flaw is that, because of the overhead lights, people *can* see in . . . and they're still doing it.

A boutique on Lexington has semi-transparent try-on chambers, reportedly to discourage shoplifting. A question of priorities.

The new Paraphernalia on 55th and Lex doesn't even ask you to come in and look. Giant slides, visible from the street, are flashed on the rear wall. The slides show pieces of girls in pieces of Paraphernalia clothes. The favorite shot is the reverse décolletage—the expanse of space between skirt and knees.

Of all the places to go to look, the discothèque is the ur-example of a voyeuristically programmed institution. It is a social model of the classic telescope situation. The looker is surrounded by darkness and anonymity at his table. The dance floor is an illuminated stage where people move in ritualistic exhibitionism. Darkness re-creates a feeling already associated with privacy and intimacy—the delight of a private world. Exhibition is instantly rewarded by constant looking.

Discothèques have been called examples of sexual detachment. Sociologists cite the seemingly uninvolved dancing patterns of two partners: "Look how asexual they are. They never touch. They rarely even look at each other." What they observed, however, was not sexual detachment but the amplification of sexuality. The feeling a discothèque generates is clearly "Why dance for one partner when everyone in the room is looking at me and I can move for all of them?"

The disco is a fine balance between voyeurism and exhibitionism. Men and women indulge in both. Women become more voyeuristic because they are stimulated by the action as dancing increasingly mimics sexuality. If you took all the clothing off all the people in a discothèque in one night and put it in a pile, there would be a lot less of it than, say, a pile of clothes from a concert. Or a supermarket. And certainly less underwear. We are in a very small moment in social time when the bra has become a very important piece of clothing not to wear. And the discothèque is *the* place not to wear it to.

In a disco, the feeling of anonymity is heightened by the isolating bombardment of sound and light. Table conversation is impossible. There is usually no restaurant ritual to follow. Each person is left to the luxury of looking.

Cerebrum, the club that was not so much a disco as a public happening, was a place implicitly geared to voyeuristic impulses. The people who thought it up would deny that. They would say that the diaphanous robes which customers don after they undress increase freedom, that group games lead to communal experience. I say it is a kinesthetic kindergarten with people constantly distributing new toys designed for self-expression; where play groups are encouraged; where the theme is what-do-we-do-next-ism; and where there are even rest periods where everyone stops his own personal grooving to lie down and watch a pale light show. The effect of nudity is either electrifying or dull. Neither sensation encourages group participation. But there's plenty to see.

Several men said they couldn't stop looking at the just-perceptible nude bodies all around them. They were turned on by the looking and not by the joining-in possibilities Cerebrum offers. For me the whole undress, self-express, dress thing was too much like what Helen Gurley Brown calls the Noontime Quickie. The figures in white gowns looked all the same and very antiseptic. But, as one friend kept telling me when we argued about it, "You're not a voyeur, you're a girl."

If personal responses and the man-woman thing are key determinants in a voyeuristic experience, what about the addition of real vs. unreal elements in movies and the theater? There is a fine line between sensual visual enjoyment and sexual enjoyment stimulated by vision. The voyeuristic purists say that no matter how visually stimulating a movie is, the whole thrill of witnessing reality is gone. The moviegoer knows he will "get to see it," and whatever titillation he feels in a movie theater has already been programmed into the film. The sensual stimulation is contrived, and this takes away the voyeur's pleasure in it.

For the purist, finding a nighttime karate class performing in some building on the corner of 72nd Street and Broadway is infinitely more rewarding than nudity in the Living Theater, no matter how spontaneous they contrive to make it. Nude performers are not by definition stimulating. The nude scene in *Hair* is, for some lookers who seek more sophisticated titillation, merely a gimmick. To others, surprised by a proscenium full of naked bodies, it is real excitement. But as a maker of exploitation flicks said, it all depends on your appetite.

## *Tom Burke*

# *THE NEW HOMOSEXUALITY*

Pity: just when Middle America finally discovered the homosexual, he died. Countless stolid burghers, reconciled to the idea of such opulent phenomena as acid rock and the male pill, are finally prepared to empathize with (if not quite approve of) this thirty-fiveish semi-neuter whom they imagine to be the prototypical modern deviate: a curio-shop proprietor with an uncertain mouth, wet basset eyes, a Coppertone tan and a miniature Yorkshire, who lives in a white and silver Jean Harlow apartment, drinks pink gin, cooks *boeuf Bourguignon,* mourns Judy, makes timid liaisons on 42nd Street, gets mugged by midnight cowboys, and masturbates while watching televised swimming meets. The public is now prepared to have a gingerly if patronizing romance with him, and, alas, the attachment is necrophilic: he has expired, with a whimper, to make way for the new homosexual of the seventies, an unfettered, guiltless male child of the new morality in a Zapata moustache and an outlaw hat, who couldn't care less for Establishment approval, would as soon sleep with boys as girls, and thinks that "Over the Rainbow" is a place to fly on 200 micrograms of lysergic acid diethylamide.

That the public's information vis-à-vis the new deviate is now hopelessly outdated is not the public's fault. It cannot examine him on its own because, from a polite distance, he is indistinguishable from the heterosexual hippie. It cannot read about him, because novelists have not written about him, and journalists concentrate on the protest actions of a handful of homosexual radicals. Television may be aware of him, but it isn't telling. Which leaves movies and the stage, the principal purveyors of a homosexual image that is at least five years behind reality. The worst recent offender is the play *The Boys in the Band* (anyone who doubts that the heartland has embraced deviation may ponder the fact that the play recently enjoyed a successful run at Caesar's Palace, Las Vegas). Its characters are touted as representative contemporary homosexuals, and are perpetuated in a carbon-copy film version, when actually they are about as pertinent to our time as the snood. As most of the world now knows, *The Boys in the Band* concerns a gay birthday party given by a thirty-year-old boy with a penchant for elaborate duplex apartments, jet-set watering holes, vicuña sweaters, hair sprays and lunches at the Oak Room of the Plaza Hotel, none of which he can afford. His eight guests all reflect his stereotyped behavior in one way or another. They eat canapés, drink excessively, do a chorus-line dance called the Madison (popular on Fire Island in the fifties), quote old movies, and imitate Judy, Bette and Kate. They submit masochistically when asked to play a game in which their collective Guilt is revealed. When they leave, their chastened host weeps a bit ("If we could just not hate ourselves so much") and exits bravely, for midnight mass. Curtain. The audience files out, feeling educated. Except for George Cassard, who smiles with irony, shakes his head, and then yawns, luxuriously.

George Cassard, who looks somewhat like Jim Morrison, and believes that he looks more like Jim Morrison than he actually does, was twenty-three on August 6, 1969, and is therefore a Leo, though his moon is in Scorpio. On the wall of his rather Spartan Chelsea cold-water flat, he has drawn, with the meticulousness of an ancient map-maker, his horoscope: the sun, moon and planets placed correctly in the twelve houses of the zodiac. "Scorpio is the sex sign," he will say, smiling enigmatically at his moon.

He is an art assistant in a staid advertising agency. He has his teeth cleaned every three months, rather than the usual six. He has read *Steppenwolf*. At home, on Long Island, he was a Boy Scout. He still collects coins. He flies kites. He is a homosexual. Through friends of friends and similar contacts, I have met a number of young men very much like him, and each has allowed me to accompany him to one of the parties he attends. The parties are nearly identical, except that George's happens to be a birthday celebration. Like the other boys, he has been told that I am a writer, but does not seem to care especially what I may write about him, or whether his name will be used. After the party, when I ask him if he would like me to make up a pseudonym for him, which, in fact, I have done, he seems mildly surprised.

"Why, man?"

"Well, your job, or your parents."

"My parents know about me. They're quite young, for parents. My dad is only forty-four. They're very hip. Very groovy, very beautiful. My mom smokes hash." He breaks off, making a curious small exhaling sound. "But she doesn't drop acid. They do worry about me dropping acid. I told them I only tripped twice, which isn't exactly true, and they know it. Anyway. What did you ask me? Oh, yeh, the job. Well, why should I pretend to be something I'm not? I mean, uh, pretend not to be something I am. They never asked me, but if they did, I wouldn't lie. How can you live a lie, man? That's not living. If they get uptight, up theirs. I don't want to work for somebody that bigoted. Print *their* name too, if you want."

He frowns and exhales again. I assume that he is reconsidering, but he says, "You're not going to put in my address, are you, or the phone or anything?"

"No, why should I?"

"Good. I mean, I don't want a lot of freaks phoning. Like I was putting a balling ad in *Screw*, or something."

George Cassard has said to meet him on the corner of Christopher Street and Greenwich Avenue at ten o'clock. From there we are to proceed to the party. At this point, we have not met, only talked on the phone, and it occurs to me that we have not discussed a way of recognizing one another in the armies of young men who idle here on a clear evening. But, without hesitation, he comes to the store window where I wait, guided, perhaps, by some sixth sense afforded him by astrology, or Boy Scouting.

"Cool," he says. He does not offer his hand. "I was afraid you might be old being a writer. Groovy. Everybody at this party will be pretty young, too." He tosses his long hair once, emphatically, as if inserting a "stop" in a telegram. It tosses minimally, because it is secured by a Cherokee beaded headband. His necklace is made of Navaho talismans. His white body-shirt looks beige, shaded by his resolutely tanned chest. A chain belt and tapestry-look bell-bottoms hang at his bony hips; a suede pouch hangs from the belt.

"You wanta smoke?" His voice seems to come from under the tanned chest. Without waiting for an answer, he produces from the pouch a joint wrapped in yellow Stella Sweet Banana Paper, lights it, and starts up Greenwich, motioning to me with his head. Follow the yellow brick road. He exhales, and a passing boy catches the scent. "Beautiful," the boy murmurs into the air, grinning straight ahead.

"Lay lady lay—lay across my big brass bed," Dylan invites from within. The walls of the loft are black; slender lengths of plumbing, painted silver, angle up them and across the ceiling. Beneath dim hanging lamps made of Sinclair Oil cans, Fresca can clusters and antique vegetable graters, on Pakistani cushions and Moroccan mats, twelve young men and four girls, all of whom look rather like Jim Morrison, sit cross-legged or recline euphorically. Leon, the guest of honor—it is his twenty-first birthday—comes forward; he is small, and grins, gnome-like, welcoming us with an ill-defined acknowledging gesture. The guests look up at us, nodding; introductions are unnecessary, made extraneous by Dylan. Joel, Leon's lover, approaches slowly, as if the smoke in the air is mildly obstructive and offers his pipe of hash, a glass of lime-colored, acid-laced Kool Aid, and the ice-cream log melting on the kitchen counter. From his suede pouch, George takes the birthday gift: a half ounce of Acapulco Gold tied in a Baggie. Leon darts his small head to George's face; it is not so much a kiss as a pleased little aside, a tiny piece of affectionate choreography. Uxoriously, he hands the Baggie to Joel, who opens it and sniffs. Joel wears only a felt outlaw's hat and a sort of loincloth. His body is offhandedly muscular as if, not long ago, he played a mild sport regularly. His legs and torso are finger-painted in rudimentary art nouveau, and on his chest is lettered, "Happy Birthday, Little Leon," and "Love" and "Peace."

* * *

A few days later, I arrange to talk to one of the guests, Jim Pasieniti, who is twenty-four, lives in the east Eighties, and commutes every morning to graduate school in New Jersey. The uptown gay bar in which he asks me to meet him is nearly empty at cocktail hour, and it bears no resemblance to the ornate, recherché homosexual habitats of *The Detective* or *The City and the Pillar.* A scruffy, well-worn room that smells of stale draft beer and billiard chalk, it could be a Bronx workingman's pub, except for the absence of American flags and girlie calendars. When Jim has ordered a Coke—he says that he almost never drinks—I ask him if he agrees with me about the party being representative.

"Yeh. Well, they don't all end like that," he says, laughing. "That happened partly because we were stoned, but dope wasn't the only reason. I mean, everybody knows that *straight* kids get into group sex these days. So do gay ones. It's very different with the older gay crowd, the guys in their forties. The orgies they have are calculated, planned things, and would never, never include women. Old fags are too inhibited for that. Don't get me wrong: younger homosexuals aren't group-groping twenty-four hours a day, but that sort of thing *is* much more prevalent. Why? Well, gay kids in their twenties don't have the hang-ups that old queens had when *they* were in *their* twenties, so they start making out much earlier, and get bored sooner with sex in pairs. So they start using poppers pretty young, and getting interested in group activities such as the baths, or in playing around in places like the Christopher Street docks, or even the subway johns, because those places are more dangerous—they're watched by the fuzz, naturally—and therefore more of a challenge. Also, those scenes are more virile, in an odd way, more masculine. They're kind of a young answer to the old guys who have to take you home very formally and mix you a martini and make a big deal of doing the traditional sex number, alone, in private. Danger is groovy. It's always new."

He chews the ice from his Coke glass thoughtfully. "Uh, I don't mean by 'masculine' and 'virile' that kids are going in for the rough, sado-masochistic sex. I think there's less of that among young guys because they're more honest with themselves than the older crowd. That leather ritual satisfies the old queen's need to prove to himself that he's a man. The young kids just don't feel that need."

I ask Jim if he knows any homosexuals of the type depicted in *The Boys in the Band* and similar efforts. He shrugs and shakes his head.

"If those queens are still around, you don't see them.

If you do, they're *really* older, like in their sixties. The summer I was eighteen—six years ago—I worked as a waiter in a gay bar. There were plenty of younger ones like that in those days. They would bring their poodles into the bar, and set drinks on the floor for the dogs to sip. Christ. There was something so lonely about them—the guys, not the dogs. They planned their whole schedules around these squeaky, high-strung little poodles that couldn't have cared less about them. Like old women with cats—something to give the days a pattern. One of them asked me up to his place for dinner. Christ, that apartment. It looked like the Castro showroom on Times Square, only not as masculine. Everything . . . *embellished.* You know: not a straight line in the whole apartment. I remember that The Beatles were still new then, but very big, and—you won't believe this—*he had never heard of The Beatles!* He had this old Ethel Merman record. And Judy Garland—everything of Judy Garland. She was interesting, but I mean, who wants to *listen* to that stuff? It's all external, while rock is, you know, internal. That theatrical music is kind of a denial of sex, while rock is *pure* sex."

He stretches, and cracks his knuckles loudly; the noise wakes the dozing bartender. "It struck me as weird, that a guy who really resented and feared women could relate only to these *female* singers—Ethel Merman and so on. Some of his buddies came up, and they drank a lot and kept arguing about how Ann Sheridan laughed. I mean, they seemed to cling to this trivia to avoid reality, which was, to them, the old guilt bit. *That's* what has died: this homosexual feeling of being isolated from the straight world by guilt. The whole country has divided into two groups: those who care about what people do in bed, and those who don't. The guilty and the guiltless. The old queens are in the first category, the kids are in the second. That's why this camp business means nothing to them. I think camp was a way for queens to distract themselves from their guilt, and today, who needs it? I'm getting pretty heavy here, you want me to go on? Okay: there used to be this syndrome of drink, guilt and camp. Now, it's dope, freedom and well, rock, and soul, and the humor of the head. Beauty, and gentleness, and love in homosexual terms used to be essentially feminine. Now, they don't have a gender. Movies were camp, and queens could only identify with women. Today, gay kids identify with males —with Peter Fonda, or Dustin Hoffman. And they aren't interested in, you know, 'theater,' or 'Broadway'—except of course *Hair*. And the whole matter of chicks. It used to be that fags couldn't relate to females that weren't mothers. Today homos think of chicks as chicks. They don't want mothers. Take the chicks at that party. About half the gay guys I know have had sex with chicks like them. . . ."

* * *

What is hard to understand is how the writer of a serious play or movie about modern homosexuals could have missed all this. Even if he shuns parties and bars, he could hardly have avoided several other symptoms of the new homosexual life-style—its political maneuvers, for instance, as reported in detail by news media since at least the middle sixties. The Mattachine Society of New York, most famous of the homophile organizations, has been getting its name in print constantly since the demise of Robert Wagner (who tended not to answer when they phoned). John Lindsay had barely been sworn in before Dick Leitsch, the Mattachine's vociferous director, rose at one of the Mayor's town meetings to denounce the entrapment of homosexuals by police. Even as he spoke, a plainclothesman was entrapping an innocent but effete young man in the back room of Julius Bar, Greenwich Village. An Episcopal minister (who had stopped in the bar for a sandwich) witnessed this, and phoned another minister, who phoned the Mayor and almost everyone else of any importance with a listed number. The result was a meeting in a village café attended by an influential *heterosexual* group that included the Mayor, the police commissioner, the police commissioner's wife, Allen Ginsberg, the Civil Liberties Union, and The Fugs. Entrapment ended the next morning.

Leitsch's next move, of course, got nationwide coverage. Attended by the press, he approached four Manhattan bars armed with a card stating his sexual persuasion and demanding service. Three places served him cheerfully; the fourth, Julius Bar, which had been serving non-card-carrying homosexuals for years, refused, and Leitsch instantly lodged a complaint with the Human Rights Commission.* Within two months, the State Liquor Authority lifted its traditional ban on homosexual bars, and, during the next two years, various state courts decided that "intrasexual" dancing, touching and even kissing were not necessarily disorderly, as long as the various sexes refrained from touching one another upon "primary sex organs." (Police who disapproved of this new climate of tolerance insisted there was a fine line between primary and secondary sex organs, and that when homosexuals danced, they frequently touched one another upon the buttocks, a possibly criminal act, since, for many deviates, the buttocks are decidedly not secondary.)

As the new milieu was being legalized, it was also being boosted by myriad aberrations of the new heterosexual

---

* *The Mattachine's highly publicized New York stand motivated similar actions in other places, but none were especially effective. In San Francisco, for example, Mattachine members who found the Society too conservative formed radical splinter groups, called SIR and, inevitably, the Pink Panthers, but their most aggressive move so far has been to protest the drafting of homosexuals, a rather frivolous ploy, since homosexuals are draft-exempt anyway.*

permissiveness: by unisex clothing, innocently born in the forties when the first bobby-soxer bought her first pair of boy's Levi's, finally labeled, sanctioned and merchandised by Seventh Avenue; by the altered straight reaction to overt gay activity in "mixed" environments such as the locker rooms of public beaches (indignation gave way to amused indifference, then marked curiosity); by the public's sympathy for Walter Jenkins during his 1964 Y.M.C.A. men's room debacle; by casual use of the terrible ten-letter word not only on television panel discussions but on prime-time network entertainments (culminating in the deviant gags now standard on every major variety program except *The King Family Presents;* by the spate of "major" gay films, especially *The Detective;* by the national burgeoning of such overt homosexual diversions as the exclusively gay pleasure boat which currently steams up the Ohio every clear weekend from the public landing at Cincinnati; by the evolution of homosexual ghetto streets from places of clandestine meeting to approximations of West Point's Flirtation Walk; and, indeed, by the sudden embracing of the film version of *The Boys in the Band* by key members of the New York power structure. Bergdorf Goodman, the Sherry-Netherland Hotel, Doubleday Bookstores, Julius Bar, the New York City Transit Authority and La Guardia Airport all consented to appear in the movie, and invitations to the somewhat fey party given to publicize it were sent out in the names of New York Society leader Mrs. William ("Chessy") Rayner, Mrs. Mortimer Hall (née Diana Lynn, movie actress turned social doyenne in the manner of Merle Oberon), and Natalie Wood. Moreover, the party was reported at length on the "Food Fashions Family Furnishings" page of the *New York Times,* along with a symphony benefit and other less-dubious galas.

While such developments were reassuring the New Homosexuality, the psychedelic life-style was giving it a form. Not that one subculture simply aped another; in point of fact, the majority of contemporary homosexuals under forty are confirmed pot-heads and at least occasional acid-trippers. For those now in their early and mid-twenties, drugs were just another part of adolescence, like The Beatles and puberty. They smoked the same grass and dropped the same acid as their heterosexual peers, but drug-oriented behavior—autistic, passive, childlike, alienated—was especially gratifying to them, partly because it so annoyed *straight* adults. Their heterosexual fellow heads, after all, though properly alienated, did maintain one important allegiance with The System: heterosexuality.

Homosexual senior citizens—anybody over twenty-nine—embrace psychedelia for an even simpler reason: the well-known homosexual compulsion to postpone old age by carefully imitating the young. The middle-aged deviate merely grows what is left of his hair very long, wears beads, body-shirts, Western vests and peace emblems, studies the head's manner of movement and speech, and goes right on getting high on alcohol, because he considers drugs unsafe. But the typical thirtyish, aspiring adolescent lays in supplies of pot, hash, etc., and makes quite a project of going on the wagon. First he smokes on weekends, then week nights. He already owns some denim bells, perhaps a string of beads, but now his building superintendent receives the stacks of collegiate chinos, the elbow-patched J. Press jackets and bleeding madras shorts, as he buys whole new wardrobes in little shops with silver walls and Mick Jagger on the stereo. As the liquor dealer misses him, so does the barber: his hair grows until eyes in the office narrow, but even that, like the selling of mutual funds itself, suddenly seems so irrelevant, while the secretary's cerulean blue cup of bright-colored pencils becomes so . . . immediate. His smiles are bemused, his laughter suddenly leprechaunish. He acquires a nickname. He buys new books: *Astrology, the Space-Age Science; The Little Prince;* the *I Ching;* Kierkegaard, and composes little private exercises in Kierkegaardian freedom—"I choose *not* to go in and sell mutual funds tomorrow, thereby recovering my freedom to *do* so." In the end, however, it is much more attractive to call in sick and stay home to read Kierkegaard, or to get up at noon, smoke, and then go shopping for black paint for the dull white apartment walls, inexpensive strobes, prisms, colored plastic boxes, aluminum paper, incense, scented candles. Life takes on a delightfully transient quality as meals become fanciful little picnics of Scooter Pies, Fresca and Tootsie Pops. Lists are made, new records purchased: Blood, Sweat & Tears, The Rotary Connection, the *2001* sound track, and *Hair,* the new deviate's only acceptable cast album.

He had frequented the handful of refined cocktail bars where the older contingent still gathers (places referred to even by their patrons as "wrinkle rooms"). Occasionally, he had stopped in the hangouts of the leather crowd, who tend to be the aged cocktail drinkers recostumed in motorcycle jackets and chains. Now, he smokes at home, puts on surplus Navy bells, and visits a bastion of the New Homosexuality on Christopher Street. All replicas of Jim Pasieniti's uptown retreat, they have retained the ambience of the neighborhood gin mill because that is how their new clientele prefers them. The lighting is harsh, the floor, the walls and the blues on the jukebox dirty. Semi-heterosexual construction-worker types mix easily with the other patrons; the pool players take their games very seriously, swaggering around the billiard table, pausing to pose slue-foot. No one holds a cigarette as if he longed for a cigarette holder.

And one head knows another; conversation is standardized.

". . . Uh, what did you say? I'm a little stoned."

"Yeh, well, so am I."

Gentle laughter.

"Uh, I was going home and smoke some more. Want to come?"

He does. Heads, though unacquainted, know that they will find so much in common. The same esoteric frame of reference, the same rather elaborate, pleasantly inventive approach to sex. Straights—nonsmokers—simply wouldn't understand. And in the light of the strobe, minds expanded, age differences, if they did exist, suddenly count for so little.

Timothy Leary and other Brahmins of psychedelia assert that LSD cures homosexuality. According to homosexuals, what it actually cures is the notion that a cure for homosexuality ought to be sought at all. But acid does seem to produce in most homosexuals a new, if somewhat ill-defined and subordinate interest in the opposite sex. "In high school, I never noticed girls," says Paul, a manly twenty-one-year-old who migrated from an Oklahoma farm to Los Angeles two years ago, and leans now on his flower-painted Volkswagen outside a Hollywood gay bar. "I guess I was afraid of them. I was uptight about everything—very serious, very heavy. When I came out here I started smoking regularly, and tripping. During my second trip, I was walking along the Strip at night, and passing these pretty girls—and suddenly, I was *smiling* at them. Wow! Oh, wow. I wasn't trying to, it just happened. On acid. The same thing happened to my two roommates. Now, there always seem to be some girls around when we go out. It's groovy. They don't seem to expect anything of us. Except it *is* a little lie, they are, uh, waiting for us to get around to them. . . ."

I give Paul my hotel phone number and a few days later he calls to take me to a party, in a run-down cottage in Laurel Canyon, hippie mecca. The walls of the house are faded cream stucco, the furnishings, motel contemporary; otherwise, the atmosphere is reminiscent of Leon's birthday. Paul loses himself in a cluster of admirers, and I speak to a remarkable girl named Joy, who wears a silver Dynel wig and says she is on speed.

"Isn't this outasight? Everybody grooving together. What? Of course they're gay. Everybody is gay. I want to sleep with every gay boy in this room. They are beautiful and I am going to lay every one of them. They make me feel more like a woman than straight squares. I hate straight pigs who treat women like pieces of meat. Say, what are you pumping me for? Are you some kind of talk freak?"

After smoking a passed joint, Paul brings the oven rack from the stove in the kitchen, ties two strings to one side of it, winds the strings around his index fingers, places his fingers in his ears, and enlists someone to "play" the rack with a metal spoon. The effect, he says, is like hearing Tibetan chimes from a great distance. When I have tried the rack, he listens politely to more questions.

"Yeh, I know some older guys. Last year, I answered a roommate-wanted ad in the paper, and the guy turned out to be forty. The 'room' turned out to be a ten-room pad in Beverly Hills. It looked like a French whorehouse. I did live there for about four months, and he never mentioned my share of the rent. But the idea of smoking grass freaked him. 'It's addictive,' he would scream. '*I* don't need that kind of escape,' he'd say, finishing a bottle of gin. He could have been sort of groovy if he'd have smoked. But he was such an old maid. He had this shelf full of books about homos where there was very little sex but a lot of crying and suffering and in the end one of the boys always killed himself. I could never figure out *why*. I brought home a copy of this groovy dirty book called *Song of the Loot. . . .*"

"Would that be '*Loon*'?"

"Yeh, *Loon,* which is all sex, and he started it and

didn't like it because it didn't have enough suffering. Such a—lady, but at the same time, a drunk. Mostly he'd just pass out and go to sleep. Wow: drink is evil. I think there ought to be some kind of law against it, like there used to be."

He stops a minute, thinking, then says: "We were talking about acid before. There's something else about it. Uh . . . well, the kind of work I do is, I'm a hairdresser. When I first got out of beauty school, in L.A., I used to bleach my hair, and, uh, wear mascara and scream a lot with the other kids."

He shakes his head at the memory; watching him now, it does seem hard to believe. "Well, acid changed that. The first trip—wow. It was the most important twelve hours of my life. I saw what I was. A fruit. And I was able to change. I just got more cool. It brought back my masculinity. The guys I live with are also hairdressers, but you'd never know it. They went through the same acid thing I did. Now one races a bike—uh, motorcycle—and the other races this old Corvette he bought. He even learned how to take a motor apart. This dike taught him. Cool?"

When I ask Paul about printing his name, he agrees readily ("I can't hide or play games, that's what screws up straight people"), then bites his thumbnail and asks if I am going to write about drugs. "Oh. Well, then I gotta say no. I am not copping out. If I lived anywhere else, I wouldn't care. But the L.A. fuzz! Four of my friends got busted for possession, just last month."

Up and down Sunset Boulevard, or Wabash Avenue, or Christopher Street, this is the common reaction. If today's homosexual is secretive about anything, it is drug use, not homosexuality. Naturally, those who are eager to declare themselves in print are still a minority, but what is significant is the surprising number who will, and the much larger number who refuse to dissemble for family or friends. The mood of belligerence has apparently spread even to homosexuals who marry. Though they are older, determinedly conservative, and excessively concerned with appearances, even they no longer seem to pretend very elaborately, either before or after marriage. Lesbians, of course, have never had to be as covert as homosexual males, simply because the Establishment has always tended to regard them merely as harmless eccentrics. (This, too, may change: the Establishment does not attend meetings of the new militant women's liberation groups.)

If this is where homosexuality is, where is it going? Where will it be in three years? Ten? "Groovier," says Jim Pasieniti. "Maybe we'll reach the Hindu ideal—man and woman united." He smiles sardonically. "Once, the good old apple-pie idea was that men and women screwed conventionally in the popular position, or abstained and took cold showers. Separately. Okay, so now 'normal' people are finding out that fellatio and cunnilingus are just as 'normal' as anything else. So doesn't it follow that the whole world is readjusting its concept of what is normal and what is perverted—and what is homo or heterosexual? Nobody *has* to be one thing or the other anymore. Even homos who are still afraid of sex with women—well, with all these nudes everywhere, how is anybody going to remain very freaked at the sight of anybody else's privates? I don't know—bisexual isn't really a valid word now, because its connotations are old-fashioned. And somebody better come up with the right word, because we're going to need it. Within ten years, we'll have the first group marriage. The communes already prophesy it, the population problem will push it along. By 1990, the old husband-and-wife unit will be nearly obsolete. First, there will be trio marriages—though the marriage ceremony will be obsolete, too—in which, say, two guys and a girl live together and all groove on each other with no specific sexual roles. After that, group living. Group grooving. It's coming."

What about "Gay Power"? Will it hasten group grooving, and the rest? "Well, you want to laugh at all that, the riots, the Gay Power meetings, and so on, but I don't know. If it gets organized, finds a leader, anything could happen."

Abruptly, he does laugh. "You know what the best bit of irony was? The riots started the night Judy Garland was buried."

It did almost seem that the New Homosexuality had picked the night to wreak havoc upon Manhattan, scorning the elder traditionalists who flew the flags on their Cherry Grove cottages at half-mast and sat home in decorous seclusion, mourning. Actually, the Village disturbance probably had nothing to do with either the death of an old homosexual idol, or the first night of the full moon. But it was significant as the most dramatic indication to date of just how aggressively the New Homosexual may speed his own evolution.

And Christopher Street had looked so routine: the usual gaggles of teen-age boys, who, though accompanied by girls, are, one must admit, distinctly *tapette* (rather as Paul of Los Angeles described himself, pre-acid); skittish old ladies walking Scotties; mobs of tourists in shorts and peaked caps. No one seems particularly interested in the quiet arrival of police at the Stonewall Inn, the street's notorious all-male private dancing club.

When the bars of the old homosexuality were raided, patrons tended to leave the scene as rapidly as possible. The Stonewall's ejected customers, however, young and belligerent, gather on the sidewalk, complaining loudly. Passers-by linger. "Pig cops!" a boy shouts, and the cry is taken up. An empty beer can strikes a patrol car, then another, then rains of cans, bottles and coins. The amazed police quickly lock themselves inside the club, as the mob charges, battering the doors with an uprooted parking meter. One boy throws lighter fluid inside the club, then a lighted match. Sirens scream as dozens of police materialize. By the time the sidewalks are cleared and the crowds dispersed, it is nearly dawn.

The next day, Saturday, the Village, all its sexes, can talk of nothing else. The police have told reporters that they closed the Stonewall only because it had refused to apply for a liquor license. This statement is widely doubted. The Mattachine Society, in a hastily mimeographed pamphlet, charges the S.L.A. and the police with renewed homosexual harassment, and vows retribution. Rumors fly up and down Christopher—that the demonstration was instigated by the S.D.S., the A.C.L.U., the Black Panthers, the White Panthers, the Pink Panthers, rival bars, and a homosexual police officer whose roommate went dancing at the Stonewall against the officer's wishes. On the club's battered facade, someone has scrawled, in chalk, "GAY POWER." The movement has a motto.

Disturbances continue for a week. Each evening by sundown the sidewalks overflow, with earnest liberal couples from uptown, with middle-aged homosexuals in from Fire Island, looking nervous and bewildered, with pugnacious pairs of young men, some holding hands, their eyes bright with new resolve. "Gay Power!" they shout, defying the swarms of Tactical Police. "Gay Power!" echo delighted neighborhood children, circling on bicycles. It is rumored that the now-ubiquitous "Equality for Homosexuals" stickers, printed by the Mattachine in snappy Day-Glow blue and fuchsia, have been attached surreptitiously by night to the patrol cars parked outside the Sixth Precinct, on Charles Street. The Stonewall, deferring to its new notoriety, strings a double strand of bright bulbs from its roof to the sign over its door. On Waverly Place, a crowd gathers to witness a sidewalk debate between a portly man in a white shirt and a boy in an acid-green tank top and long unkempt red hair tangled like a fright wig. The man seems to be trying to speak for his Village neighbors, heterosexual; he has been talking to everyone on the block, he is saying, and the straight residents sympathize with the oppressed homosexual, but the boy will not listen. "The hell you say!" he shouts. "You don't impress me. *You* are straight and *you* are my enemy! Don't give me that phony liberal bull. *You* made the laws! Nixon's silent army!"

The audience laughs. He leans close to his opponent, his face turning deep red. "Now *we* are gonna get *you!*"

The man looks ashen, quite frightened. Clearly, he would like to escape, but fears the boy's reaction.

"I was in Vietnam, man, how does that grab you? Huh? Huh? Two Congressional Medals! And, man, I'll screw your daughter. *But I'll screw your son first!*"

He does not appear at the town meeting called by the Mattachine after the July Fourth weekend, but he is there in spirit. It is to be an open forum, held in St. John's in the Village Episcopal Church, on Waverly, in a huge, low-ceilinged room, its floors gently scarred by countless chicken suppers. The air is heavy and unwelcoming, like that of a winter-clothes closet opened in summer. Rows of funeral-parlor chairs hold at least two hundred people, most of them male, and young. They fan themselves with Mattachine handbills, yawning; the proceedings have not begun auspiciously. A thin, motherly woman stands before them, introduces herself as Mrs. Cervantes, the Mattachine's secretary, and says that Dick Leitsch will be late.

"Now I, personally, am not gay," she continues, smiling as if she addresses a garden club or cooking class, "but believe me, *your* cause is *my* cause."

"*What* cause?" an older man with yellow-gray curls whispers sideways. His friend, who holds a tiny, agitated terrier in his lap like a muff, shrugs, making a *moue*. The whites of his eyes are gin-red. What, they seem to be asking, are these children so concerned about? *We* are satisfied with things as they are. Our bars have always been raided. It is our cross. We go to other bars, and, like Judy, keep on smiling. What are *we* doing here? There must be an *All About Eve* revival somewhere in town. *What* cause?

Dick Leitsch, in a staid brown suit, strides to the front. From a distance, he looks somewhat like a dependable, fortyish Cartier salesclerk. Mrs. Cervantes steps aside. With professional aplomb, he reopens the meeting. Police brutality and heterosexual indifference must be protested, he asserts; at the same time, the gay world must retain the favor of the Establishment, especially those who make and change the laws. Homosexual acceptance will come slowly, by educating the straight community, with grace and good humor and . . .

A tense boy with leonine hair is suddenly on his feet. "We don't want acceptance, goddamn it! We want respect! Demand it! We're through hiding in dark bars behind Mafia doormen. We're going to go where straights go and do anything with each other they do and if they don't like it, well, *fuck them!* And if some of us enjoy a little group sex at the docks or in the subways we're going to have it without apologizing to anybody! Straights don't have to be ashamed of anything sexy they happen to feel like doing in public, and neither do we! We're through cringing and begging like a lot of nervous old nellies at Cherry Grove!"

The men with the terrier wince. So does Dick Leitsch.

"We're going to protest in front of St. Patrick's," another boy calls. "The Catholics have put us down long enough!"

"If every homosexual in New York boycotted Bloomingdale's, they'd be out of business in two weeks!"

"Well, now, *I* think," says Mrs. Cervantes, "that what we ought to have is a gay vigil, in a park. Carry candles, perhaps. A peaceful vigil. I think we should be firm, but just as amicable and sweet as . . ."

"*Sweet!*" The new speaker resembles Billy the Kid. He is James Fouratt, New Left celebrity, seminarian *manqué*, a radical who burned real money on the floor of the New York Stock Exchange as a war protest.

"Sweet! *Bullshit!* There's the stereotype homo again, man! Soft, weak, sensitive! Bullshit! That's the role society has been forcing these queens to play, and they just sit and accept it. We have got to radicalize, man! Why? Because as long as we accept getting fired from jobs because we are gay, or not being hired at all, or being treated like second-class citizens, we're going to remain neurotic and screwed up. No matter what you do in bed, if you're not a man out of it, you're going to be screwed up. Be proud of what you are, man! And if it takes riots or even guns to show them what we are, well, that's the only language that the pigs understand!"

Wild applause. The handbills fall to the floor. Dick Leitsch tries to reply, but Fouratt shouts him down.

"All the oppressed have got to unite! The System keeps us all weak by keeping us separate. Do you realize that not one straight radical group showed up during all those nights of rioting? If it had been a black demonstration, they'd have been there. We've got to work together with *all* the New Left."

A dozen impassioned boys are on their feet, cheering. They are the new radicals who will rally in Washington Square, and lead a mass march down Sixth Avenue, halting astonished traffic, carrying the lavender "Gay Power" banner, chanting "Gay Power to Gay People," singing *We Shall Overcome* solemnly in Sheridan Square.

Again and again, Dick Leitsch tugs frantically at his clean white tie, shouting for the floor, screaming for order. He is firmly ignored.

## *Paul Bindrim*

---

# *NAKED THERAPY*

KEN: I think Lou said it much better . . . I was not so much inhibited as scared of my reaction to other people, and of course scared to death of having an erection.

MURRAY: I particularly enjoyed looking at the bodies of the women, at their genitals and breasts.

SANDRA: Normally I don't find that looking at a nude man is particularly exciting, but I thought you guys really looked great in the light show. It really brought out a lot of the strength, and I thought "that looks like what a man ought to look like."

LOUISE: I found myself thinking. "Do I look as good as her?" Comparing, and I didn't particularly like that reaction, and I felt like kicking myself for doing it, but I *was* doing it, and I thought, "I'm kind of fat here, and this and that, and do I want it to be out in the open and out in the light and have someone looking at me and thinking the same things about me?" This kind of bothered me, especially when I was looking at Anita. She has such a lovely body.

LEO: I enjoyed the lovely female bodies last night. Many of your breasts—I wanted to touch them, feel them, put my face against them.

These remarks were made by participants at various times during a nude marathon. I've begun with them in order to get whatever sensationalism there might be about a nude encounter group not only out in the open but also out of the way.

The basic marathon is a period of no less than twenty hours of intimate, intensive, authentic human interaction, uninterrupted by subgrouping, eating or sleeping. Such round-the-clock pressure leads the participants to take off their social masks, stop playing games, and start communicating openly and authentically. In theory, anyway, a marathon group moves from mistrust to trust, from polite acceptance to genuine critique, from Peeping-Tomism to participation, from dependency to autonomy, from autocracy to democracy. During this trial by intimacy, one's roles, masks and pretenses tend to peel away layer by layer, revealing a more authentic self.

As emotional intimacy develops in clothed groups marathon members have shown a spontaneous tendency to disrobe. On one occasion when a swimming pool was available participants swam in the nude after the marathon. These spontaneous excursions into nudity seem to indicate that personal isolation and estrangement had been reduced.

Naturally enough, some of us wondered what would happen if marathon members first disrobed, and then interacted. Abraham Maslow, former president of the American Psychological Association, raised this question in *Eupsychian Management.* "I wonder what would happen if these encounter groups remained exactly as they are but only added a physical nudism." Later he defended nude marathons when they were attacked on ethical grounds, making possible the continuation of this research. Perhaps the whole process of becoming emotionally open and intimate would be hastened and intensified by nudity.

In addition most people in interacting groups—as well as in society—hesitate to touch each other. To touch is to be intimate, and to be intimate in that curious Henry

Jamesian sense is to want or to have sexually. If full body contact between nude men and women were to be encouraged, and yet sexual expression prohibited, might this not lead more quickly to a sense of emotional intimacy and a sense of intensified personal identity that is the goal of all marathon groups?

(The wonderful Margaret Altmann has said of tourists throwing stones at her beloved wapiti elk that there is usually no malice or desire to hurt involved, but simply a thwarted desire to make contact with something elusive, strange, free and beautiful. How many of us have not been in that position vis-à-vis other human beings?)

The results of the experimental marathon I'll be talking about in this article were good, and they thus help answer the question, why a *nude* marathon? Seventeen of the twenty participants felt that they had opened up to each other on more authentic and meaningful levels as a result of nudity; of the remaining three, none felt that nudity had hindered his ability to interact. Those clinical psychologists who participated felt that the group had integrated and become therapeutically functional more rapidly than participants had at clothed marathons they had attended. Five weeks after the marathon, fifteen of the participants gathered at Long Beach State College and reported beneficial changes in themselves and in their relationships with members of their families, colleagues and the world in general. These changes were the result generally of increased self-confidence and self-expression, diminished fears of rejection, decreased anger or hostility toward one's own faults, and a readier and more levelheaded overall acceptance of other persons.

But let me now fill in some of the details: how the marathon was set up, who the participants were, what they did, where they did it, etc. My co-sponsor of this experiment, Dr. William E. Hartman, professor of sociology at California State College at Long Beach, and I sent out announcements of the proposed nude marathon to psychologists, marriage counselors, participants in group and individual therapy, and persons who had attended typical marathons clothed.

Of the ten men and ten women who were selected for our marathon there were three engineers, two schoolteachers, four clinical psychologists, one pharmacist, two magazine editors, two social workers, one artist and five housewives. There was one married couple, and, although some married persons came without their mates, most of the participants were single.

We met at the Deer Park nudist camp near Escondido, California. Deer Park is large; it affords privacy in a beautiful natural setting. Its facilities include a swimming pool and a swirling hot Jacuzzi bath large enough for our entire group. Since the camp had just been closed to the public, the marathon had complete privacy.

The twenty participants agreed to:

1. Stay with the group for the entire session and avoid subgrouping;
2. Participate in all scheduled activities;
3. Remain in the presence of nude persons, and feel free to remove one's clothes or not;
4. Use first names only, if they wished;
5. Abstain from alcoholic beverages and drugs throughout the session;
6. Refrain from overt sexual expression. Hugging and kissing would be permissible, but not the fondling of genitals or intercourse;
7. Take no photographs.

The group was in continuous session from 9:00 P.M. Friday until 3:00 P.M. Sunday, with six hours out each night for sleeping. Meals were served cafeteria style.

The participants were asked beforehand to bring with them the things they most enjoyed smelling, touching, tasting, looking at, and hearing, for use as stimuli in a sensory-saturation experience designed to induce a peak state perhaps best described as a mild turn-on.

It is probably simplest to describe the relevant events of the marathon in a straightforward, day-by-day narrative. By relevant events I mean those relating to the new factor or vector of nudity. Therapeutic interactions of the sort typical in clothed marathons took place as well, of course.

FRIDAY

The group met on Friday evening with all members clothed. Everyone was asked to share with the group his anxieties, anticipations and fantasies about social nudity. Participants were again assured that they did not have to strip. This interaction took a little over an hour. The session then moved to the bath and members were told that they could bathe in the nude or otherwise, as they chose; everyone chose to bathe nude. The session in the bath was followed by an experience with colored lights in the main meeting room. Those who wished to participate actively stood in front, where colored patterns were thrown onto their bodies by a 35-mm slide projector; they could scrutinize the beautiful patterns and colors in a full-length mirror. Those who preferred to observe sat quietly in the darkened room. After the colored light session, the group retired for the night.

SATURDAY

After an hour's walk around the grounds and then breakfast, members were asked at the day's opening session to share their impressions of Friday's activities. This session was held out of doors, and was tape-recorded. Members' responses may be summarized under the following headings.

*A sense of pleasure from the freedom to look at bodies of others and to be looked at in return.* The colored light session permitted overt expression of voyeuristic and exhibitionist tendencies, of course. (As the marathon continued, the tendency to look excessively, or to experience self-consciousness when being looked at, declined almost to the point of disappearance.)

*A sense of personal comfort, exhilaration, and freedom.*

*The desire to touch and a sense of being inhibited in this desire.* There was little skin contact in the Friday session in the baths. Members were particularly aware of their reluctance to touch and repeatedly asked themselves why.

*A sense of group closeness.*

*Relief and surprise among the men at their not having become unduly aroused sexually.*

*A sense of guilty concern about one's body.* Members became, in retrospect, very aware of their negative feelings about their bodies—among the men there was concern whether their penises were large enough, and among both men and women there was a concern whether they were paunchy, or flabby, or wrinkled, whether they were as good-looking as certain other members, and so on. This concern about looks later dissolved or at least abated markedly; certain members commented that it seemed to come in part from movie and magazine stereotypes. Members increasingly felt themselves to be right and beautiful, each in his own way, and forgot about *Playboy* and movie stars.

*The experience of being high or at least unable to sleep for most of the night.* The various exhilarations, worries, surprises, etc. seemed to give everyone something to think about and kindled a feeling of success exciting enough to keep him awake.

After lunch, another encounter was held in the Jacuzzi bath, followed by an hour of movement and sensory awareness, led by Sara McClure, a dance therapist. There was another brief bathing period in the evening. Full body contact became more spontaneous, particularly in the warm water of the pool, and less sexually centered. Dance therapy furthered this process.

SUNDAY

The Sunday morning session included an hour of meditation with sensory-saturation. Each member, after prolonged periods of looking into the eyes of potential partners, selected as a partner a member of the opposite sex with whom eye contact was most comfortable and relaxing. Each member was then seated close to and facing the person of his choice. All were then asked to close their eyes and keep them closed. The prelude to Wagner's *Tristan und Isolde* was played. During this period, each member was asked to touch, taste and smell simultaneously the items he had selected for this experience. (One participant touched velvet, ate chocolate, and smelled a rose.) This sense-saturation led to a mild, drugless peak state or high.

While he was in this state, each participant was asked to reexperience in fantasy the best moment of his life—a wonderful happening or experience in which he had felt joyous, free, close to the heart of his being, and at one with the world. When he had completed his fantasy recall and was turned on to his limit, each member was asked to touch fingertips with his partner's, and to gaze quietly into his partner's eyes. After twenty minutes of eye-centered meditation, members were asked to place their chairs in a circle and share their experiences.

Most of the participants felt that the periods of sensory-saturation, fantasy and eye-centered meditation were the most profound experiences of the marathon. The general outlines of this experience are not unlike those of drug-induced, hypnotic or Zen-meditational trips. Many members reported a sense of going out, a traveling through and beyond the boundaries of ordinary experience and an approach to something variously called "God," "warm, white light," "birth," "the beauty of the whole thing," "the stream of the universe," "a white nirvana," and so on. These experiences seemed to have a lasting effect on the post-marathon attitudes and behavior of many of the participants. An increased sense of inner worth, a sense of having completed a crucial psychic or spiritual cycle, helped some to a better understanding of their marriage partners. (In one case this expressed itself as an amicable divorce. In another, a remarkably beautiful woman whose husband had made childish and petulant fun of her body, was able to get her husband to stop playing little boy and to move the entire relationship onto a much more stable, mature and mutually satisfying level.) Several men and women reported that for the first time in years they had had friendly and adult relations with persons of the opposite sex.

The success of the peak experience encounter on Sunday was, I believe, strongly prepared for and mediated by the prior therapeutic experience of social nudity.

The tentative conclusions that I reached from this first nude marathon were encouraging. I reasoned that just as a lack of tender, tactile contact seems to be responsible in certain cases for infant deaths, the same deprivation may produce a nonlethal but chronic tension and anxiety among adults. That is, controlled skin contact might be therapeutic in and of itself. Perhaps the social world is such a jungle of polite estrangement that sensory isolation may create a famine in the heart that cannot be relieved by any *one* person, even one's mate. If purely physical contact (particularly between males who are most strongly inhibited in this respect) remains tenderly sensual yet takes place within an environment in which goals of a purely sexual nature have been deconditioned, then perhaps genuine mental and emotional exposure and acceptance can flower more naturally and more beautifully.

Self-acceptance, I reasoned, is often associated with one's body image. Open exposure to group reaction in the nude state might often remedy purely imaginary distortions, thereby increasing ego-strength and empowering men and women to make more honest and more salutary struggles with their core emotional problems.

Since sensual body contact is often a primary way of expressing oneself emotionally and of responding adequately to others, and since our culture defines sensuality and sexuality as bed-mates, perhaps we have blocked vital avenues of communication that might easily be reopened.

While such speculations are rather heady to have been based mainly on one experimental encounter involving twenty carefully selected participants, my initial conclusions continue to be verified. Since that first Deer Park marathon, I have held thirty-eight nude marathons. New techniques, drawn from my original theories, have increased the effectiveness of the sessions.

Sensitivity training has been criticized—and rightly—for the use of untrained and unsupervised leaders, for neither screening applicants nor providing follow-up, and for not testing its theories. None of these objections applies to the nude marathons I conduct. Half of the participants already have been pre-screened in a sense, for they have been referred by other psychologists and psychiatrists. In addition, each participant is screened preliminarily by telephone and must agree to regard the first part of the marathon itself as a screening process, with the understanding that if I ask him to leave, he will go immediately. While this is not ideal, it serves as a compromise between the excessive costs of pre-testing and the blind commitment to work with just anyone who shows up for a marathon. All participants attend a follow-up session, and I am always available for private consultation. Testing is under way.

Opposition to nude marathons continues from the uninformed and from those who are threatened by the thought of removing their own clothing. Accusations of gimmickry, manipulation and publicity-seeking have been made by some psychologists.

Conflicting viewpoints are common in the field of psychotherapy where few therapeutic techniques have been adequately tested. Only solid data can hope to settle these questions. Fortunately, academic psychologists have become interested in nude marathons as broad-spectrum learning experiences and a number of research projects are being planned. One project at the Center for Behavior Therapy in Beverly Hills will attempt a more definitive behavioral analysis of nude marathons.

Qualified therapists who participate in nude sessions share my own optimism. The method has spread rapidly in spite of strong social pressures. Among the twenty-nine therapists now conducting nude marathons are the presidents of the Los Angeles Society of Clinical Psychologists and the American Association for Humanistic Psychology.

Examples of benefits from the nude encounter continue to multiply, though the nude marathon is still too new for long-term follow-up and evaluation. Frigid females, impotent males and sexual exhibitionists have become at least temporarily symptom-free. Arthritics have been relieved of pain. Long-standing bachelors who could not commit themselves emotionally have married. Depressed individuals have been freed of suicidal tendencies. Psychotics in remission have lost their compulsive gestures and behaved normally by the end of a session. Swingers at one nude marathon found a new need for emotional relatedness in sexual expression. Marriages have been revitalized.

Is it any wonder that, both as therapist and as scientific reporter, I remain optimistic and thrilled about the possibilities of this new therapeutic technique?

*Joe Mancini*

# *BODY PAINTING:*

# *THE YOUNGEST PROFESSION*

Body painting is as American as Andy Warhol.

Body painting is Goldie Hawn, bikinied, bugalooing on *Laugh-In*. It's the picture of a reclining nude that's become a pop-poster classic. It's a scrawny *Vogue* model with a flower on her forearm or a butterfly on her cheek.

Body painting is Kusama. Everybody knows Kusama. She's the Japanese artist who keeps giving the *Daily News* an excuse to put bare asses on page one by staging body-painting spectaculars in public.

Body painting is an ad in the underground press promising:

*Something Different*

"Young, lovely boy & girl models for nude sketching, photography and skin painting."

And body painting is Lois Kaplan.*

Lois is a twenty-one-year-old high school dropout who likes to talk about a career in jazz dancing. But she makes her living as a body-painting model. She makes a very meager living out of body painting—about fifty dollars a week. She makes a very good living on the side. Her basic rates:

Intercourse: $50

---

* The name has been changed.

Fellatio: $25

"The guy comes into the studio and asks to skin paint," Lois explains. "He pays the boss twelve dollars for half an hour or twenty dollars an hour. Then I get him alone. Once the door is shut behind us, I make my own deal. The boss gets none of it. The guy usually makes the first move. He tells me he's not really interested in body painting, and I ask him what he's interested in. If he's shy, I know how to come on. I know how to talk to a hippie. I know how to talk to a businessman. Before I'm through, he's telling me, 'Wow, you're really dynamite.'

"I give it to them straight and never change my price—take it or leave it. But I think some of the girls, if they need the money or are uptight about their attractiveness, do it for as little as $5. We don't rap to each other about prices, though, so I don't know.

"Because I charge so much, I get lots of requests for blow-jobs. It seems strange to some people, but I don't mind blow-jobs and won't give hand-jobs. I don't like them.

"If the customer wants to touch me or jerk off, the price is $15. I can't charge any more because they'd just go into the bathroom and take care of it themselves. You'd be surprised how many idiots pay just to sit in a room with me naked and jerk off."

Lois must be worth the money: she's already become a favorite at the Times Square studio where she's been working just a few months. She draws the boss's special customers—judges, lawyers and police brass. (The police are paid off in trade—and cash—which explains why her studio has been raided only once while Lois herself remains a statutory virgin—she has yet to experience her first bust.)

A visit to a body-painting studio can be a costly adventure. A customer might spend close to one hundred dollars after paying twenty dollars to the house, fifty dollars to the higher-priced model and (as most of Lois' regulars do) tipping over and above the set rate.

Aside from the nitty-gritty, Lois must decorate the studio's waiting room seven hours a day in skimpy underwear, baby-doll pajamas or a topless bikini. Or she can sit around naked. "I don't like clothes anyway," she says. For an exhibitionist like Lois, who earns extra pocket money posing for spread books (publications that skirt the edges of legality by cramming their pages with spread-eagled nudes), ritualistic nudity can be an added dividend.

But the life of the skin model is, of course, basically hard work. In the first place, the physical surroundings are not always geared to her comfort.

"The room is large and air-conditioned," says Lois, "but there's just one metal chair and a posing platform made of bare, solid boards. The customer doesn't mind because he's too excited to notice and he's usually on top. But after a good day, my back really aches."

Then there's the acting performance. Feigning sexual pleasure in the embrace of a paunchy, perspiring police captain is about as liberating as a hair shirt. "These guys pant and moan and I've got to pant and moan," says Lois. "They think they're giving you such a thrill. If they only knew. I could be shampooing my hair while they're working their wonders on me."

There are other occupational hazards. One evening, a distinguished looking man in a three-piece business suit doffed his jacket and asked Lois to turn around and bend over, leaving her bra and pants on. "I thought he was just an ass freak. There are plenty of them around," she says. "But as I bent over, sticking my ass out at him, I got a premonition." She spun around and caught a stinging belt buckle on the side of her face.

Can a canvas scorn its artist? It's not quite that simple. Because of the hairy incidents that are her stock and trade, the body-painting model has veto power over her clients.

Lois tells of a recent example: It was shortly after five o'clock and a pungent, eye-watering canopy of cigarette smoke was settling over the studio anteroom. Lois had just started the night shift and the after-work crowd was beginning to trickle in. That meant sweaty, middle-aged businessmen, assuming transparent poses of nonchalance, stealing furtive glances at her barely-covered body as they stammered their requests for a skin-painting session.

An ancient hulk was staring at her from the other end of the room. His eyes skimmed from the model to her nude photo on the wall. "Hey Lois," he read the name from a sign above the photo, "would you like me to paint your body?"

One signal from Lois and her boss informed the man that she was booked for the rest of the night.

Lois has been in body painting only six months. She is a New York girl who dropped out of a vocational school in Rego Park, Queens, four years ago (at seventeen), got married and had it annulled four months later. She tried dancing in Wisconsin summer stock, became a garment center showroom model and finally drifted into the East Village crash-pad style of love.

Inevitably, Lois met Simon Minelli,* the well-publicized East Village swell who had his finger into, among other things, the body-painting pie. Simon had lots of girl friends and used them all, at one time or another, as poser-prostitutes in his East Village studio. The trouble with selling the chicks you're balling, he learned, is that as soon as they split your pad, they split your studio. When he met Lois, he desperately needed fresh young talent. Without hesitation, she joined his entourage.

---

* The name has been changed.

"Simon was close to the fuck papers and that crowd," she says. "He used to circulate the tale that if you wanted a girl, any kind of girl to do anything you wanted, he could arrange it. He'd get as much as one hundred dollars and give the girl maybe twenty dollars. Simon is a rat."

So Lois went to work for the uptown studio, where she commands considerably more than twenty dollars a throw. "In an ordinary job as a secretary or waitress, you have to work from nine to five, put up with a lot of hassles and go home every week with eighty dollars or ninety dollars after taxes," says Lois. "Here, I get my share of hassles but, working six good days, I can make more than $1000, tax free. It's the easiest way I know to make that kind of money."

It's the easiest way a lot of girls know. Hundreds of nude photography sketching and skin-painting models pose-and-lay-for-pay in these studios, located mostly in Times Square, Chelsea and the East and West Villages. Characterized by a common lack of sexual scruples, they gravitate to Manhattan, attracted by the magnetic marathon of easy living and easy money. They are, almost without exception, young, good-looking and well-stacked.

"They've increased my business tenfold," says one studio owner who used to oversee a stable of streetwalkers. "These girls can talk to the customers, make them feel like they're making the scene. Make them feel like they're balling the type of with-it chick you read about every day."

Moonbeam is one of them. She's twenty-four, pug-nosed, baby-faced, with freckles, dark electric hair and heavy breasts. She works in Greenwich Village.

"I get some weirdos," she says. "Last week I had a customer, all he wanted to do was jerk off. As soon as I got my clothes off, he started to jerk off.

"Then there was the guy who just wanted to hug me. I liked him. He was nice.

"One winner got his jollies by fooling around with my breasts. He kept asking me if I ever had any children and sometimes he would call me momma."

Moonbeam insists she's quit laying for the customers (at the insistence of her boy friend). "My old man didn't mind me selling my body," she explains, "except when I did dumb things. He really got mad one day when a guy came near my face and I got some sort of disease. I was sort of blowing him and you can get diseases that way. That's why I stopped doing dumb things."

Voyeurs, mammary maniacs, oral-genital freaks, sado-masochists and even foot fetishists. "I had a foot fetishist once," relates Josie, an uptown model. "He paid fifteen dollars to lick my toes. It's like a very weird feeling. But it's kind of pleasant, too."

These are not the only draws. One customer, a thirty-seven-year-old architect, spends about two hours a week in a body-painting studio. He gets a massage. "I like a rub-down by a naked girl whose company I enjoy," he says. "This is the only way I can get it. So I give twenty dollars to the studio, another twenty-five dollars to the girl, and I get what I want."

There are even those who come to body paint. "I don't dig having my body smeared with paint," shrugs one model. "And I don't understand what the customer sees in it, either. But they tip well, too."

Sometimes the body painters are the oddest of all: Two middle-aged men, believed to be Texas oil millionaires, spend four days a week in New York—Thursday through Sunday. Every Friday without fail, each rents a room in an uptown studio. From noon to 10 P.M., a stream of models parades into these rooms. The oilmen dance, sing, hum and paint. They paint hamburgers, steaks and chops. Not cartoon renderings of hamburgers, steaks and chops. Realistic hamburgers, steaks and chops. In water-color. With Daliesque draftsmanship.

"The only thing besides meat I've ever seen them paint is maps," says a model. "They're good on maps. They painted a map of Europe on me once. One of my nipples was Florence and the other was Naples. They're very talented."

Counting hourly fees, bonuses to the studio and tips to the models, these oilmen splurge about $1000 apiece each week to touch up tenderloins while rehearsing a song-and-dance routine.

At last count (the number fluctuates according to the legal and financial fortunes of the owners), more than half of New York City's six or seven body-painting studios were good old-fashioned whorehouses. But even in these, for every model that does, there's a model that won't, at least not until she knows her customer well enough to be certain he's not an undercover cop.

But what about the boys?

Where male models are concerned, body painting and prostitution are almost totally synonymous. One man who uses the service regularly explains it this way:

"The male trade is one of the oldest—and least talked about—businesses in this city. It used to be a strictly word-of-mouth affair. You patronized a service, got satisfaction and told your friends about it. But the quality of boys has gone down. They're not as beautiful as they used to be and they don't know how to treat a customer. It's a very demanding profession to work for a male service. A good hustler can't be effeminate and, to really turn on his customer, he's got to have a superior air about him, even an arrogance. The really proficient ones are scarce these days.

"The only alternative for a lonely homosexual, who's perhaps getting a little frayed around the edges, used to be the gay bars. But the young boys who hang out in those places are either not up to snuff or, if they are, they're in it for sex. They lay for other young, beautiful boys.

"Then the body-painting studios started advertising

in the underground papers. They'd give names and physical descriptions of their boys and you could call up and ask for a model by name. Most of the time they'd even send the boy over to your place for a private session.

"The first time I tried one of the studios I was amazed. The boy came over and he was great. He was young, he was handsome and he had a great body. Just like the old days. Body painting has replaced male service in this town."

A model gives his version: "We do what we have to. I don't know of any male body-painting model who doesn't give some sort of sex to his customer. They blow or get blown, they masturbate or get masturbated, and very few are squeamish about anal intercourse, whether it's on the giving or receiving end.

"But I've found that the better model is the one who does the least sexually. I'm bisexual. I've done everything there is to do in my private life with men or women. But I can truthfully say that I've never blown a customer and I've never been buggered by a customer.

"You learn that sex is the least important thing in their minds. What they really want is someone to communicate with. You have to know how to listen. Make them feel somebody cares. Make them leave feeling, 'Well, that's an hour out of my life that I wish more of my hours were like.' "

For every skin-painting bordello, there's a pristine palace where the painting of naked bodies is the only sensualism sanctioned. Claude Brickell, sandy-haired, tousled and twenty-three, is co-owner of The Gallerie, a legitimate body-painting studio in a loft on 18th Street just east of Fifth Avenue. An earnest young man, Claude is apparently sincere in his devotion to body painting as a pop-art form.

"We're trying to upgrade body painting here," he says. "That's why we charge a little more (fifteen dollars a half hour, twenty-five dollars an hour). Our models, male and female, are all attractive in face and form. The other places are amateur and trying to be professional. We want to be professional but we'll also serve the amateurs. We attract our share of oglers, but we don't cater to the voyeur trade. We're also planning to branch out and become an agency for nude models."

Claude's partner is Denise Bell, twenty, a buxom blonde in the Marilyn Monroe tradition, who once ended up as a nude, body-painted birthday present at a surprise party in Scarsdale. The suburban assignment (without any sexual fillips) netted the studio $50 and two black lights, which came in handy at The Gallerie, where Day-Glow paint is used.

Denise and Claude, who modeled together at a Greenwich Village studio, say they decided to go into business for themselves after watching their former boss haul in the cash.

Despite the lack of sexual inducements, The Gallerie is doing well, especially for a place open only since the beginning of the summer. Voyeurs and artists, lechers and photographers, writers and undercover cops have passed through its portals. And even men on a busman's holiday:

A customer emerged smiling from a private session recently, thanked everyone and left. Seconds later, his model, a slender girl called Kitty, came out wrapped in a towel. "Do you know who that was?" she laughed. "Remember all the trouble I had when I had the baby? That was one of the doctors who worked on me. A gynecologist.

"I have an infection and he spent the end of the session looking at it and telling me I must come in and have it seen to."

Claude Brickell spends most of his working day on the telephone. "I sometimes get calls where the customer lays it on the line," he says. " 'Listen,' they tell me, 'I want a girl who puts out.' I always answer the same way: 'If that's what you want, why don't you go to a bordello?'

"They know that if they go to a bordello, they have to perform. In a body-painting studio, they can rationalize. They feel they're part of the now generation and if they get laid, too . . . Well, that's part of the whole scene."

A large, shabby man in his mid-thirties lumbered into the studio, sweat-soaked forelocks clinging to his brow. Huskily, he whispered to Claude that he was interested in skin painting. Claude suggested that he choose a model. There were six of them.

"It's embarrassing to select them when they're sitting right here," he mumbled.

"It would be more embarrassing if there were only a couple of them," Claude answered softly.

The man settled on one, a voluptuous dark-haired girl, and they withdrew to a body-painting chamber. About ten minutes later, he emerged alone, an almost psychotic anger in his eyes. He stumbled toward the door, glaring at everyone in the room. Finally, without a word of protest, he staggered out.

Claude shook his head. "That happens often," he said. "When they discover there's nothing except body painting, they don't want to use up their hour. They don't want to look, they don't want to paint. They just want to go.

"Those other studios are giving us a bad name," he sighed.

Good or bad, "those other studios" *are* giving body painting a name. Consider the recent case of one young Manhattan bachelor who won an especially sweet poker pot.

"I really feel terrible about this," he told his poker partners as he raked in the cash—about fifty dollars. "But I've got to leave soon."

His friends suggested he spend the proceeds in some

way that would benefit all of them. One, who had earlier been scanning the ads in an underground newspaper, had an idea: "Why don't you go to a body-painting studio? Then you'd have to report to us—in detail—what really goes on in those places."

In minutes, the man who had dreamed up the scheme had a studio on the phone. It was between 10:30 and 11 P.M. "Are you still open?" he asked.

Shortly, the guinea pig was at the studio, a second-floor loft divided by partitions. In the anteroom, five models—three girls and two boys—sat on a pair of studio couches. "You want a girl, right?" asked a bespectacled, fortyish man.

"Yes. How much is it again?"

"Well, it's twenty dollars an hour for each person, but if you take two it's only thirty-five dollars." The customer chose a bell-bottom-trousered blonde girl and a brown-haired boy in blue jeans. The boy immediately took charge.

"This way," he said, ushering them into a medium-sized room lit by a single ceiling lamp and decorated by one wall of gleaming tinfoil. Crammed into a corner was an over-stuffed, coarsely-covered mattress.

"My name is Tony," said the boy, apparently about nineteen. The girl, who looked the same age, said nothing.

"Where are the paints?" the customer asked.

"Not everybody comes here to body paint," replied Tony. "You're not really interested in body painting, are you . . . ? Why don't we take off our clothes?"

Tony shed his jeans and sweatshirt. Underneath, he was naked. The girl unbuttoned her white blouse, revealing small, uplifted breasts. In one motion, she peeled off her bell bottoms and panties. She was slender, sylph-like, unblemished.

"Take off your clothes," Tony urged.

"I want her to undress me," said the customer. She complied, quickly, expertly.

"Okay, what's your bag?" Tony wanted to know as the trio moved to the mattress.

Throughout the encounter, the girl performed with submissive but dispassionate efficiency. Tony seemed to enjoy his work. Incredibly, they never set a price. Not before and not after. In all, it had cost the customer forty-five dollars—thirty-five dollars to the studio and five dollars tip each to Tony and the girl.

The next night, when the customer reported back to his poker partners, the response was sensational. One man immediately got on the phone to ask for a minor variation.

"I want two blondes, see," he told the man. "And they've got to be the flooziest blondes you can dig up. Plenty of make-up."

"But what if we can't get two blondes?" the studio asked.

"Then get them wigs," he demanded.

The customer got his blondes. No wigs, either.

*George Steiner*

---

# *NIGHT WORDS: HUMAN PRIVACY AND HIGH PORNOGRAPHY*

Is there any science-fiction pornography? I mean something *new*, an invention by the human imagination of new sexual experience? Science fiction alters at will the coordinates of space and time; it can set effect before cause; it

---

[Controversy over this article (which originally appeared in *Encounter*) continued for many months, and is continuing still. My knowledge of and interest in pornography are, I would suppose, no greater than the middle-class average. What I was trying to get into focus is the notion of the "stripping naked" of language, of the removal from private, intensely privileged or adventurous use, of the erotic vocabulary. It does seem to me that we have scarcely begun to understand the impoverishment of our imaginings, the erosion into generalized banality of our resources of individual erotic representation and expression. This erosion is very directly a part of the general reduction of privacy and individual style in a mass-consumer civilization. Where everything can be said with a shout, less and less can be said in a low voice. I was also trying to raise the question of what relation there *may* be between the dehumanization of the individual in pornography and the making naked and anonymous of the individual in the totalitarian state (the concentration camp being the logical epitome of that state). Both pornography and totalitarianism seem to me to set up power relations which must necessarily violate privacy.

Though the discussion which followed on publication has been heated, neither of these two issues has, I feel, been fully understood or engaged.]

works within a logic of total potentiality—"all that can be imagined can happen." But has it added a single item to the repertoire of the erotic? I understand that in a forthcoming novel the terrestrial hero and explorer indulges in mutual masturbation with a bizarre, interplanetary creature. But there is no real novelty in that. Presumably one can use anything from seaweed to accordions, from meteorites to lunar pumice. A galactic monster would make no essential difference to the act. It would not extend in any real sense the range of our sexual being.

The point is crucial. Despite all the lyric or obsessed cant about the boundless varieties and dynamics of sex, the actual sum of possible gestures, consummations, and imaginings is drastically limited. There are probably more foods, more undiscovered eventualities of gastronomic enjoyment or revulsion than there have been sexual inventions since the Empress Theodora resolved "to satisfy all amorous orifices of the human body to the full and at the same time." There just aren't that many orifices. The mechanics of orgasm imply fairly rapid exhaustion and frequent intermission. The nervous system is so organized that responses to simultaneous stimuli at different points of the body tend to yield a single, somewhat blurred sensation. The notion (fundamental to Sade and much pornographic art) that one can double one's ecstasy by engaging in coitus while being at the same time deftly sodomized is sheer nonsense. In short: given the physiological and nervous complexion of the human body, the number of ways in which orgasm can be achieved or arrested, the total modes of intercourse, are fundamentally finite. The mathematics of sex stop somewhere in the region of *soixante-neuf;* there are no transcendental series.

This is the logic behind the *120 Days*. With the pedantic frenzy of a man trying to carry pi to its final decimal, Sade labored to imagine and present the sum total of erotic combinations and variants. He pictured a small group of human bodies and tried to narrate every mode of sexual pleasure and pain to which they could be subject. The variables are surprisingly few. Once all possible positions of the body have been tried—the law of gravity does interfere—once the maximum number of erogenous zones of the maximum number of participants have been brought into contact, abrasive, frictional, or intrusive, there is not much left to do or imagine. One can whip or be whipped; one can eat excrement or quaff urine; mouth and private part can meet in this or that commerce. After which there is the gray of morning and the sour knowledge that things have remained generally the same since man first met goat and woman.

This is the obvious, necessary reason for the inescapable monotony of pornographic writing, for the fact well known to all haunters of Charing Cross Road or pre-Gaullist bookstalls that dirty books are maddeningly the same. The trappings change. Once it was the Victorian nanny in high-button shoes birching the master, or the vicar peering over the edge of the boys' lavatory. The Spanish Civil War brought a plethora of raped nuns, of buttocks on bayonets. At present, specialized dealers report a steady demand for "WS" (stories of wife-swapping, usually in a suburban or honeymoon resort setting). But the fathomless tide of straight trash has never varied much. It operates within highly conventionalized formulas of low-grade sadism, excremental drollery, and banal fantasies of phallic prowess or feminine responsiveness. In its own way the stuff is as predictable as a Boy Scout manual.

Above the pulp line—but the exact boundaries are impossible to draw—lies the world of erotica, of sexual writing with literary pretensions or genuine claims. This world is much larger than is commonly realized. It goes back to Egyptian literary papyri. At certain moments in Western society, the amount of "high pornography" being produced may have equaled, if not surpassed, ordinary belles-lettres. I suspect that this was the case in Roman Alexandria, in France during the *Régence,* perhaps in London around the 1890's. Much of this subterranean literature is bound to disappear. But anyone who has been allowed access to the Kinsey library in Bloomington, and has been lucky enough to have Mr. John Gagnon as his guide, is made aware of the profoundly revealing fact that there is hardly a major writer of the nineteenth or twentieth century who has not, at some point in his career, be it in earnest or in the deeper earnest of jest, produced a pornographic work. Likewise there are remarkably few painters, from the eighteenth century to post-Impressionism, who have not produced at least one set of pornographic plates or sketches. (Would one of the definitions of abstract, non-objective art be that it cannot be pornographic?)

Obviously a certain proportion of this vast body of writing has literary power and significance. Where a Diderot, a Crébillon *fils,* a Verlaine, a Swinburne, or an Apollinaire writes erotica, the result will have some of the qualities which distinguish his more public works. Figures such as Beardsley and Pierre Louÿs are minor, but their lubricities have a period charm. Nevertheless, with very few exceptions, "high pornography" is not of pre-eminent literary importance. It is simply not true that the locked cabinets of great libraries or private collections contain masterpieces of poetry or fiction which hypocrisy and censorship banish from the light. (Certain eighteenth-century drawings and certain Japanese prints suggest that the case of graphic art may be different; here there seems to be work of the first quality which is not generally available.) What emerges when one reads some of the classics of erotica is the fact that they too are intensely conventionalized, that their repertoire of fantasy is limited, and that it merges, almost imperceptibly, into the dream-trash of straight, mass-produced pornography.

In other words: the line between, say, *Thérèse Philosophe* or *Lesbia Brandon* on the other hand, and *Sweet Lash* or *The Silken Thighs* on the other, is easily blurred. What distinguishes the "forbidden classic" from under-the-counter delights on Frith Street is, essentially, a matter of semantics, of the level of vocabulary and rhetorical device used to provoke erection. It is not fundamental. Take the masturbating housemaid in a very recent example of the Great American Novel, and the housemaid similarly engaged in *They Called Her Dolly*. . . . From the point of view of erotic stimulus, the difference is one of language, or more exactly—as verbal precisions now appear in high literature as well—the difference is one of narrative sophistication. Neither piece of writing adds anything new to the potential of human emotion; both add to the waste.

Genuine additions are, in fact, very rare. The list of writers who have had the genius to enlarge our actual compass of sexual awareness, who have given the erotic play of the mind a novel focus, an area of recognition previously unknown or fallow, is very small. It would, I think, include Sappho, in whose verse the Western ear caught, perhaps for the first time, the shrill, nerve-rending note of sterile sexuality, of a libido necessarily, deliberately, in excess of any assuagement. Catullus seems to have added something, though it is at this historical distance nearly impossible to identify that which startled in his vision, which caused so real a shock of consciousness. The close, delicately plotted concordance between orgasm and death in Baroque and Metaphysical poetry and art clearly enriched our legacy of excitement, as had the earlier focus on virginity. The development in Dostoevsky, Proust, and Mann of the correlations between nervous infirmity, the psychopathology of the orgasm, and a special erotic vulnerability is probably new. Sade and Sacher-Masoch codified, found a dramatic syntax for, areas of arousal previously diffuse or less explicitly realized. In *Lolita* there is a genuine enrichment of our common stock of temptations. It is as if Vladimir Nabokov had brought into our field of vision what lay at the far edge, in Balzac's *La Rabouilleuse*, for instance, or what had been kept carefully implausible through disproportion (*Alice in Wonderland*). But such annexations of insight are rare.

The plain truth is that in literary erotica as well as in the great mass of "dirty books" the same stimuli, the same contortions and fantasies, occur over and over with unutterable monotony. In most erotic writing, as in man's wet dreams, the imagination turns, time and time again, inside the bounded circle of what the body can experience. The actions of the mind when we masturbate are not a dance; they are a treadmill.

Mr. Maurice Girodias would riposte that this is not the issue, that the interminable succession of fornications, flagellations, onanisms, masochistic fantasies, and homosexual punch-ups which fill his *Olympia Reader* are inseparable from its literary excellence, from the artistic originality and integrity of the books he published at the Olympia Press in Paris. He would say that several of the books he championed, and from which he has now selected representative passages, stand in the vanguard of modern sensibility, that they are classics of post-war literature. If they are so largely concerned with sexual experience, the reason is that the modern writer has recognized in sexuality the last open frontier, the terrain on which his talent must, if it is to be pertinent and honest, engage the stress of our culture. The pages of the *Reader* are strewn with four-letter words, with detailed accounts of intimate and specialized sexual acts, precisely because the writer has had to complete the campaign of liberation initiated by Freud, because he has had to overcome the verbal taboos, the hypocrisies of imagination in which former generations labored when alluding to the most vital, complex part of man's being.

Writing dirty books was a necessary participation in the common fight against the Square World . . . an act of duty.

Mr. Girodias has a case. His reminiscences and polemics make sour reading (he tends to whine); but his actual publishing record shows nerve and brilliance. The writings of Henry Miller matter to the history of American prose and self-definition. Samuel Beckett's *Watt* appeared with Olympia, as did writings of Jean Genet, though not the plays or the best prose. *Fanny Hill* and, to a lesser degree, *Candy* are mock-epics of orgasm, books in which any sane man will take delight. Lawrence Durrell's *Black Book* seems to me grossly overrated, but it has its serious defenders. Girodias himself would probably regard *Naked Lunch* as his crowning discernment. I don't see it. The book strikes me as a strident bore, illiterate and self-satisfied right to its heart of pulp. Its repute is important only for what it tells us of the currents of homosexuality, camp, and modish brutality which dominate present "sophisticated" literacy. Burroughs indicts his readers, but not in the brave, prophetic sense argued by Girodias. Nevertheless, there can be no doubt of the genuineness of Girodias' commitment or of the risks he took.

Moreover, two novels on his list *are* classics, books whose genius he recognized and with which his own name will remain proudly linked: *Lolita* and *The Ginger Man*. It is a piece of bleak irony—beautifully appropriate to the entire "dirty book" industry—that a subsequent disagreement with Nabokov now prevents Girodias from including anything of *Lolita* in his anthology. To all who first met Humbert Humbert in *The Traveller's Companion Series,* a green cover and the Olympia Press's somewhat mannered typography will remain a part of one of the high moments of contemporary literature. This alone should have spared Mr. Girodias the legal and financial harryings by which Gaullist Victorianism hounded him out of business.

But the best of what Olympia published is now available on every drugstore counter—this being the very mark of Girodias' foresight. The *Olympia Reader* must be judged by what it actually contains. And far too much of it is tawdry stuff, "doing dirt on life," with only the faintest pretensions to literary merit or adult intelligence.

It is almost impossible to get through the book at all. Pick it up at various points and the sense of *déjà-vu* is inescapable ("This is one stag-movie I've seen before"). Whether a naked woman gets tormented in Sade's dungeons (*Justine*), during Spartacus' revolt (Marcus Van Heller: *Roman Orgy*), in a kinky French *château* (*The Story of O*), or in an Arab house (*Kama Houri* by one Ataullah Mordaan) makes damn little difference. Fellatio and buggery seem fairly repetitive joys whether enacted between Paris hooligans in Genet's *Thief's Journal*, between small-time hustlers and ex-prizefighters (*The Gaudy Image*), or between lordly youths by Edwardian gaslight in *Teleny*, a silly piece attributed to Oscar Wilde.

After fifty pages of "hardening nipples," "softly opening thighs," and "hot rivers" flowing in and out of the ecstatic anatomy, the spirit cries out, not in hypocritical outrage, not because I am a poor Square throttling my libido, but in pure, nauseous boredom. Even fornication can't be as dull, as hopelessly predictable, as all that.

Of course there are moments which excite. *Sin for Breakfast* ends on a subtle, comic note of lewdness. *The Woman Thing* uses all the four-letter words and anatomical exactitudes with real force; it exhibits a fine ear for the way in which sexual heat compresses and erodes our uses of language. Those, and I imagine it includes most men, who use the motif of female onanism in their own fantasy life will find a vivid patch. There may be other nuggets. But who can get through the thing? For my money, there is one sublime moment in the *Reader*. It comes in an extract (possibly spurious?) from Frank

Harris' *Life and Loves.* Coiling and uncoiling in diverse postures with two naked Oriental nymphets and their British procuress, Harris is suddenly struck with the revelation that "there indeed is evidence to prove the weakness of so much of the thought of Karl Marx. It is only the bohemian who can be free, not the proletarian." The image of Frank Harris, all limbs and propensities ecstatically engaged, suddenly disproving *Das Kapital* is worth the price of admission.

But not really. For that price is much higher than Mr. Girodias, Miss Mary McCarthy, Mr. Wayland Young, and other advocates of total frankness seem to realize. It is a price which cuts deep not only into the true liberty of the writer, but into the diminishing reserves of feeling and imaginative response in our society.

The preface to the *Olympia Reader* ends in triumph:

> Moral censorship was an inheritance from the past, deriving from centuries of domination by the Christian clergy. Now that it is practically over, we may expect literature to be transformed by the advent of freedom. Not freedom in its negative aspects, but as the means of exploring all the positive aspects of the human mind, which are all more or less related to, or generated by, sex.

This last proposition is almost unbelievably silly. What needs a serious inquiry is the assertion about freedom, about a new and transforming liberation of literature through the abolition of verbal and imaginative taboos.

Since the *Lady Chatterley* case and the defeat of a number of attempts to suppress books by Henry Miller, the sluice gates stand open. Sade, the homosexual elaborations of Genet and Burroughs, *Candy, Sexus, L'Histoire d'O* are freely available. No censorship would choose to make itself ridiculous by challenging the sadistic eroticism, the minutiae of sodomy (smell and all) which grace Mailer's *American Dream.* This is an excellent thing. But let us be perfectly clear why. Censorship is stupid and repugnant for two empirical reasons: censors are men no better than ourselves, their judgments are no less fallible or open to dishonesty. Secondly, the thing won't work: those who really want to get hold of a book will do so somehow. This is an entirely different argument from saying that pornography doesn't in fact deprave the mind of the reader, or incite to wasteful or criminal gestures. *It may, or it may not.* We simply do not have enough evidence either way. The question is far more intricate than many of our literary champions of total freedom would allow. But to say that censorship won't work and should not be asked to is *not* to say that there has been a liberation of literature, that the writer is, in any genuine sense, freer.

On the contrary. The sensibility of the writer is free where it is most humane, where it seeks to apprehend and re-enact the marvelous variety, complication, and resilience of life by means of words as scrupulous, as personal, as brimful of the mystery of human communication as the language can yield. The very opposite of freedom is cliché, and nothing is less free, more inert with convention and hollow brutality, than a row of four-letter words. Literature is a living dialogue between writer and reader only if the writer shows a twofold respect: for the imaginative maturity of his reader, and, in a very complex but central way, for the wholeness, for the independence and core of life, in the personages he creates.

Respect for the reader signifies that the poet or novelist invites the consciousness of the reader to collaborate with his own in the act of presentment. He does not tell all because his work is not a primer for children or the retarded. He does not exhaust the possible responses of his reader's own imaginings, but delights in the fact that we will fill in from our own lives, from resources of memory and desire proper to ourselves, the contours he has drawn. Tolstoy is infinitely freer, infinitely more exciting, than the new eroticists when he arrests his narrative at the door of the Karenins' bedroom, when he merely initiates, through the simile of a dying flame, of ash cooling in the grate, a perception of sexual defeat which each of us can relive or detail for himself. George Eliot is free, and treats her readers as free, adult human beings, when she conveys, through inflection of style and mood, the truth about the Casaubon honeymoon in *Middlemarch,* when she makes us imagine for ourselves how Dorothea has been violated by some essential obtuseness. These are profoundly exciting scenes, these enrich and complicate our sexual awareness, far beyond the douche-bag idylls of the contemporary "free" novel. There is no real freedom whatever in the compulsive physiological exactitudes of present "high pornography," because there is no respect for the reader, whose imaginative means are set at nil.

And there is none for the sanctity of autonomous life in the characters of the novel, for that tenacious integrity of existence which makes a Stendhal, a Tolstoy, a Henry James tread warily around his own creations. The novels being produced under the new code of total statement shout at their personages: strip, fornicate, perform this or that act of sexual perversion. So did the S. S. guards at rows of living men and women. The total attitudes are not, I think, entirely distinct. There may be deeper affinities than we as yet understand between the "total freedom" of the uncensored erotic imagination and the total freedom of the sadist. That these two freedoms have emerged in close historical proximity may not be coincidence. Both are exercised at the expense of someone else's humanity, of someone else's most precious right—the right to a private life of feeling.

This is the most dangerous aspect of all. Future historians may come to characterize the present era in the West as one of a massive onslaught on human privacy, on the delicate processes by which we seek to become our own singular selves, to hear the echo of our specific being. This onslaught is being pressed by the very conditions of an urban mass-technocracy, by the necessary uniformities of our economic and political choices, by the new electronic media of communication and persuasion, by the ever-increasing exposure of our thoughts and actions to sociological, psychological, and material intrusions and controls. Increasingly, we come to know real privacy, real space in which to experiment with our sensibility, only in extreme guises: nervous breakdown, addiction, economic failure. Hence the appalling monotony and *publicity*—in the full sense of the word—of so many outwardly prosperous lives. Hence also the need for nervous stimuli of an unprecedented brutality and technical authority.

Sexual relations are, or should be, one of the citadels of privacy, the nightplace where we must be allowed to gather the splintered, harried elements of our consciousness to some kind of inviolate order and repose. It is in sexual experience that a human being alone, and two human beings in that attempt at total communication which is also communion, can discover the unique bent of their identity. There we may find for ourselves, through imperfect striving and repeated failure, the words, the gestures, the mental images which set the blood to racing. In that dark and wonder ever renewed both the fumblings and the light must be our own.

The new pornographers subvert this last, vital privacy; they do our imagining for us. They take away the words that were of the night and shout them over the rooftops, making them hollow. The images of our love-making, the stammerings we resort to in intimacy, come prepackaged. From the rituals of adolescent petting to the recent university experiment in which faculty wives agreed to practice onanism in front of the researchers' cameras, sexual life, particularly in America, is passing more and more into the public domain. This is a profoundly ugly and demeaning thing whose effects on our identity and resources of feeling we understand a little as we do the impact on our nerves of the perpetual "sub-eroticism" and sexual suggestion of modern advertisement. Natural selection tells of limbs and functions which atrophy through lack of use; the power to feel, to experience and realize the precarious uniqueness of each other's being, can also wither in a society. And it is no mere accident (as Orwell knew) that the standardization of sexual life, either through controlled license or compelled puritanism, should accompany totalitarian politics.

Thus the present danger to the freedom of literature and to the inward freedom of our society is not censorship or verbal reticence. The danger lies in the facile contempt which the erotic novelist exhibits for his readers, for his personages, and for the language. Our dreams are marketed wholesale.

Because there were words it did not use, situations it did not represent graphically, because it demanded from the reader not obeisance but live echo, much of Western poetry and fiction has been a school to the imagination, an exercise in making one's awareness more exact, more humane. My true quarrel with the *Olympia Reader* and the genre it embodies is not that so much of the stuff is boring and abjectly written. It is that these books leave a man less free, less himself, than they found him; that they leave language poorer, less endowed with a capacity for fresh discrimination and excitement. It is not a new freedom that they bring, but a new servitude. In the name of human privacy, enough!

*Kenneth Tynan*

---

# DIRTY BOOKS CAN STAY

It's always pleasant to see prudery knocked, and whenever I read articles by fellow-intellectuals in defense of pornography, I do my best to summon up a cheer. Lately, however, the heart has gone out of my hurrahs. The old adrenalin glow has waned. And now that I've analyzed a number of recent anti-censorship tracts, I think I know why. *The writers are cheating.* A whiff of evasiveness, even of outright hypocrisy, clings to their prose: too much is left unspoken, or unadmitted. Their arguments, when you look at them closely, shift on the quicksands of timidity. On the surface, a fearless libertarian has come forth to do battle with the forces of reaction. But between the lines he is usually saying something like this:

(a) I hate censorship in all its forms, but that doesn't mean that I actually like pornography.

(b) In fact, I don't even approve of it, except when I can call it "erotic writing" and pass it off as literature.

(c) I wouldn't go into a witness box to defend it unless it had educational, artistic or psychiatric value to make it respectable.

(d) I read it only in the line of duty, and feel nothing but pity for those who read it for pleasure.

(e) Needless to say, I never masturbate.

Such—once you've stripped off the rhetoric—is the accepted liberal viewpoint; and safer than that you can hardly play. At best, it adds up to a vaguely progressive gesture that could never endanger the author's moral standing or give his wife a moment's worry. From first to last he remains socially stainless and—to me, anyway—utterly unreal. He is like a man who loathes whorehouses in practice but doesn't mind defending them in principle, provided that they are designed by Mies van der Rohe and staffed by social workers in Balenciaga dresses.

At this point I had better offer a definition. By pornography I mean writing that is exclusively intended to cause sexual pleasure. I am not talking about novelists like D. H. Lawrence or Henry Miller; sex is often their theme, but titillation is never their main objective, and if they happen to arouse us, we keep ourselves resolutely zipped, aware that what we are feeling is only an incidental part of a large literary design. (This, of course, can be fairly frustrating at times. In *Lady Chatterley's Lover,* for instance, Lawrence has a teasing habit of getting the reader tumescent and suddenly changing the subject from sex to the dreadful side effects of the Industrial Revolution.) Nor am I concerned with the Anglo-Saxon exiles in Paris who used to concoct spare-time pornography under pseudonyms for the Olympia Press; straight smut wasn't their métier, and too often they strayed from the purpose at hand into irrelevant gags and other flights of asexual fancy. *Candy,* by Terry Southern and Mason Hoffenberg, is a brilliant example of pseudo-pornography, praised by the liberal critics precisely because it was too funny to be sexy. As the porter in *Macbeth* said of drink: "It provokes the desire, but it takes away the performance."

What we are discussing is something different—hard-core pornography, which is orgasmic in intent and untouched by the ulterior motives of traditional art. It has a simple and localized purpose: to induce an erection. And the more skillfully the better. Contrary to popular myth, it takes discipline and devotion to be a first-rate pornographer, and only the subtlest command of rhythm and repetition will produce ideal results. These usually take the form of solo masturbation—usually, but not invariably, since vocal excerpts from bawdy books can often be employed to vary or intensify the customary fun of sexual coupling. In any case, the aim of pornography is physical enjoyment. Yet the liberals, at heart, disdain it, and the public as a whole seems eager to burn it. I think it deserves a few words of exculpation and thanksgiving.

In 1962 John Osborne wrote a short and startling play called *Under Plain Cover.* It dealt with a happily married suburban couple named Jenny and Tim, whose private life is entirely given up to the acting out of sexual fantasies. Sometimes she dresses up as a nurse, and he plays the apprehensive patient; in another version of the game he is a strict master threatening to punish a slovenly housemaid. They are both obsessed by Victorian knickers (English for panties), of which they have a unique collection. After one fetishistic session, they meditate as follows:

Jenny: Do you think there are many people like us?
Tim: No. Probably none at all, I expect.
Jenny: Oh, there must be some.
Tim: Well, yes, but probably not two together.
Jenny: You mean just one on their own?
Tim: Yes.
Jenny: How awful. We are lucky.

Pornography is expressly designed for those who are not, in Jenny's sense, "lucky." If your taste is for earrings or high heels or spanking or any of the other minority appetites, you may have trouble finding a like-minded bedfellow. You will be "one on their own," and that can create a strangulating sense of guilt. Pornography loosens the stranglehold and assuages the solitude; you know, at least, that you are not alone. Having bought a book that matches your fantasy, you emerge from the store with a spring-heeled stride and a surge of elation. I have felt that radiant contentment, and so have you—*hypocrite lecteur, mon semblable, mon frère*. If chance denies you the right partner, that book and others like it will be your lifelong companions. Just as old habits die hard, old hards die habits.

The erotic minority man is not alone in needing the aid and comfort of pornography. Worse by far is the plight of those who are villainously ugly and unable to pay for the services of call girls. (If they are rich, their problem is negligible; beauty, after all, is in the eye of the stockholder.) To be poor and physically unappetizing is to be sexually condemned to solitary confinement, from which pornography offers the illusion of release. And we mustn't overlook its more commonplace uses. For men on long journeys, geographically cut off from wives and mistresses, pornography can act as a portable memory, a welcome shortcut to remembered bliss, relieving tension without involving disloyalty. And for uncommitted bachelors, arriving alone and short of cash in foreign cities where they don't speak the language, hard core is practically indispensable.

It's difficult to be an enemy of pornography without also disapproving of masturbation. In order to condemn the cause, it is logically necessary to deplore the effect. A century ago, when it was generally believed that self-stropping led to loss of hair, blindness and mental paralysis, I could have understood this attitude. Nowadays, I find it as baffling and repugnant as when I first encountered it, at the age of fourteen. The debating society at my school was discussing the motion: "That the present generation has lost the ability to entertain itself."

Rising to make my maiden speech, I said with shaky aplomb: "Mr. Chairman—as long as masturbation exists, no one can seriously maintain that we have lost the ability to entertain ourselves." The teacher in charge immediately closed the meeting. Today his successor would probably take a more tolerant view. But the old prohibitions still persist.

In a recent letter to the London *Sunday Times,* a respected liberal clergyman wrote: "To be sexually hungry is the fate of thousands, both young and old. There is nothing evil in this hunger, but it is hard to bear. To have it stimulated when it cannot be honorably satisfied is to make control more difficult."

Here, in three short sentences, all the puritan assumptions are on parade—that sexual deprivation is the normal state of affairs, that it is morally desirable to grin and bear it, and that masturbation is a dishonorable alternative.

Because hard core performs an obvious physical function, literary critics have traditionally refused to consider it a form of art. By their standards, art is something that appeals to such intangibles as the soul and the imagination; anything that appeals to the genitals belongs in the category of massage. What they forget is that language can be used in many delicate and complex ways to enliven the penis. It isn't just a matter of bombarding the reader with four-letter words. As Lionel Trilling said in a memorably sane essay on the subject:

> I see no reason in morality (or in aesthetic theory) why literature should not have as one of its intentions the arousing of thoughts of lust. It is one of the effects, perhaps one of the functions, of literature to arouse desire, and I can discover no ground for saying that sexual pleasure should not be among the objects of desire which literature presents to us, along with heroism, virtue, peace, death, food, wisdom, God, etc.

That is the nutshell case for pornography as art. It could hardly be stated more concisely, and I have yet to hear it convincingly refuted. If a writer uses literary craft to provoke sexual delight, he is doing an artist's job. It is for him to decide whether four-letter words will help or hinder his design. C. S. Lewis, a great literary critic and Christian apologist, once jolted me by saying that he objected to venereal monosyllables mainly because they were anti-aphrodisiac; from antiquity onward, the best writers had found that the oblique approach to sex paid higher erotic dividends. ("The direct approach," he told me, "means that you have to resort to the language of the nursery, the gutter or the medical textbook. And these may not be the associations you wish to evoke.") But that is a question of taste. Whatever technique the writer employs, we are entitled to judge the end product as a work of art. And the basic criterion, in the case of pornography, is whether or not it succeeds in exciting us. If it doesn't, we can write it off as an artistic failure.

Lawyers, as I discovered a couple of years ago, are not impressed by the Trilling doctrine. The English distributors of *Fanny Hill* were being prosecuted for obscenity, and the publishers' legal advisers asked me whether I would appear as a witness for the defense. I said I'd be delighted. And what form (they inquired) would my evidence take? I replied by pointing out that under English law obscenity is permissible as long as it has redeeming artistic merits; I considered erotic titillation a legitimate function of art, and therefore proposed to defend *Fanny Hill* on the ground that it was expertly titillating. The lawyers' professional smiles froze on their faces. They didn't exactly throw me out, but they made it arctically clear that I would not be called on to testify. In terms of courtroom tactics, they may have been right; it's just conceivable, however, that they missed a chance of establishing (or at least of testing) a new legal precedent. In any event, they lost the case.

But I mustn't lurch into the trap of suggesting that pornography is defensible only when it qualifies as art. It is defensible in its own right and for its own sake, no matter whether it is art or not, and whether it is well or badly written. Freedom to write about sex must include the freedom to write about it badly. Some of the younger critics—

guerrillas at the gates of the literary Establishment—would go further and argue that pornography is not only different from art but in some respects more important. A reviewer in the *International Times,* London's underground newspaper, recently declared:

> In the brave new world of sexuality, perhaps we can forget about art, and read Henry Miller as he was meant to be read: as the writer whose craft describes intercourse better than anybody else's. If we have learned nothing else from Genet, we can be sure of this: his result may have been art, but that's not as important as his intention, which was pornography.

Very few critics, even today, can write about hard core without tremors of prejudice and preconception. You can sense them worrying all the time about what their readers will think of them; it mustn't be suspected that they enjoy it, because that would imply that they masturbate. So they get defensively jocose, or wearily condescending. They indulge in squirms of pity for those who actually go out and buy the stuff—the sort of pity that is twin brother of contempt. Of course, the hellfire preachers of popular reviewing don't bother with such petty qualms; for them, all pornography is subversive filth and ought to be destroyed unread. It's only in the work of intelligent critics that you hear the special tone of veiled liberal distaste, which is rather like that of a lecturer on toxicology who feels compelled to reassure us, every few seconds, that he has never actually poisoned anyone. This tone is audible even in *The Other Victorians* by Steven Marcus, a much-praised and often perceptive study of pornography in nineteenth-century England. The author is an Associate Professor of English at Columbia. Let me list some of the errors, ambiguities and critical confusions that I detect in his book:

1) Overdependence on Freudian dogma. Professor

Marcus prefaces his text with the famous quotation in which Freud proclaims that "the grandest cultural achievements . . . are brought to birth by ever greater sublimation of the components of the sexual instinct." In other words, the less energy you invest in sex, the more likely you are to produce a work of art. This is a hypothesis with no scientific basis of any kind. It is rather like saying that if you hoard enough milk, it may somehow turn into wine. The whole theory reeks of hidden puritanism, not to say magic.

2) Overaddiction to Freudian symbolism. Describing a Victorian handbook on pornography, Professor Marcus points out that its author often hangs a page of footnotes onto a single line of text. He adds that "one is tempted" to see in this "an unconscious iconography: beneath a very small head there is attached a very large appendage." Resist the temptation, Marcus: this is sub-Freudian tittering at its coyest. Later on, the professor quotes from a pornographer who casually—and to avoid repeating himself—uses the word "evacuation" to mean ejaculation. "If one expands the metaphor," Marcus comments with poleaxing pedantry, "one begins to see that the penis then might be either a fecal column or the lower end of the alimentary tract out of which fecal matter is to be expelled, the woman's body, particularly her genitals, becomes a toilet, etc." Watch out for expanding metaphors, Marcus, especially if they're anal. Again, when a hard-core hero, busily undressing a girl, says that he "unveiled beauties enough to bring the dead to life," the professor insists that the phrase is an unconscious reference to the author and his readers: *they* are the dead who need to be brought to life. If clichés can legitimately yield interpretations like that, we enter a minefield every time we uncover our typewriters.

3) Verbal snobbery, i.e., the assumption that the sexual act is inherently too ignoble to be described in noble

words. When a pornographer writes about "that inner sovereignty or force, within my balls," Marcus gets witheringly scornful: "An 'inner sovereignty' that is yet 'within my balls' is hopeless and impossible. Sovereignty is toppled from its throne by being so located—there is nothing majestic about such an urgency." This reminds me of a telling exchange at the Old Bailey in 1960, when *Lady Chatterley's Lover* was being tried for obscenity. Counsel for the prosecution, an Old Etonian and veteran of the Coldstream Guards, read a passage from the novel in tones of frigid derision and then asked Richard Hoggart, a young scholar giving evidence for the defense, whether he seriously contended that it was possible to feel "reverence for a man's balls." "Indeed, yes," said Hoggart, with quiet compassion for the fellow's obtuseness. He made it seem so obvious; and as he spoke you could feel the case swinging in Lawrence's favor.

4) Facile generalization, based on sloppy research. This crops up in the brief, disdainful chapter that Marcus devotes to the vast Victorian literature of flagellation. In books of this genre, he says, "what goes on is always the same. A person is accused of some wrongdoing. This person is most often a boy. . . . The accuser is almost invariably some surrogate for his mother. . . . An adult male figure, father or schoolmaster, occurs very infrequently." In fact, the victim is usually a girl, and male accusers are just as common as female. The professor's reading list must have been curiously selective.

5) Moral censure masquerading as stylistic disapproval. Marcus has a habit of attacking pornography in particular on grounds that apply to literature in general. At one point, for instance, he quotes a sentence that makes cloudy use of epithets such as "voluptuous," "amorous" and "tumultuous." He goes on to say that, because they are vague and unspecific, "they express an important tendency in pornography." Nothing of the sort: what they ex-

press is a tendency that exists in bad writing of any kind. Foggy prose is no more abhorrent in pornography than in Norman Vincent Peale.

But for all his lapses, Marcus is at least trying to be an objective witness, and often he succeeds. The roughest frontal assault on hard core in recent years has come from George Steiner, a sprightly American don who teaches at Churchill College, Cambridge. It was launched in an essay called "Night Words," * which Steiner contributed to the English magazine *Encounter*. He begins by contending that, since the number of sexual positions and combinations is limited, pornography is doomed to ultimate monotony. To which one replies that dawn and sunset are likewise limited, but that only a limited man would find them monotonous.

Already, quite early in the piece, there are signs that Steiner is easily bored. With a stoic yawn, he says that after any kind of sexual fulfillment "there is the grey of morning and the sour knowledge that things have remained fairly generally the same since man first met goat and woman." (Why grey instead of flesh-pink? Why sour rather than sweet? Why goats anyway?) Hereabouts he takes a sudden swerve that brings him into head-on collision with Professor Marcus, who is approaching from the opposite direction. According to Steiner, one of the definitions of abstract art is "that it cannot be pornographic." According to Marcus, pornography is "in reality very abstract."

Steiner now zeros in on his target. Reasonably enough, he maintains that there is no essential difference between "erotic writing" and hard core except in the matter of verbal sophistication. But from this he argues that neither category "adds anything new to the potential of human emotion; both add to the waste." An assumption is

---

* *Editor's note:* See previous chapter.

buried here, and I trust you dig it: what Steiner means by waste is masturbation. A long passage follows in which he easily demolishes the pretensions of Maurice Girodias, founder of the Olympia Press, who is forever protesting that what he published was not pornography but art. (My own complaint would be that although it was sometimes good art, it was always lousy pornography.) This section is dotted with words like "bore," "boredom," "repetitive" and "dull," just in case you are in any doubt about Steiner's attitude toward the desirability of writing about physical lovemaking. For what he is leading up to is nothing less than blanket condemnation of all attempts to put the sexual act into words. He asserts that the best novelists leave sex in the wings; they stop at the bedroom door. To support his case he cites Tolstoy and George Eliot, both of whom lived at a time when it was forbidden to go further. As for modern outspokenness: "There is no real freedom whatever in the compulsive physiological exactitudes of present 'high pornography,' because there is no respect for the reader whose imaginative means are set at nil." Sex is a private citadel to be jealously guarded, an experience in which two human beings must find for themselves the mental images that will set their blood to racing in dark and wonder ever-renewed. (I am compressing, but not all that much.) "The new pornographers," Steiner warns us dourly, "subvert this last, vital privacy; they do our imagining for us."

*They do our imagining for us.* It sounds like a fearful affront a chilling premonition of 1984; but in fact it is exactly what all good writers have done since the birth of literature. The measure of their talent has immemorially been their ability to make us see the world through their eyes. If they can heighten our perceptions, we should thank them, not resent them. And on the matter of privacy: I don't think Steiner is seriously suggesting that commando groups of scribbling voyeurs are going to burst into our bedrooms and take notes. We can always keep our sex lives to ourselves if we wish. But that doesn't mean (why should it?) that we must shrink from reading about other people's.

Steiner's climactic point is that hard core has no respect for "the sanctity of autonomous life" as far as its characters are concerned. They don't exist in their own right, independent and self-sustaining, like people in Stendhal and Henry James. Pornographers, he says, "shout at their personages: strip, fornicate, perform this or that act of sexual perversion." The error here is one we have already noted in Marcus: Steiner is damning bad pornography for a crime that it shares with all bad fiction. Incompetent writers *always* shout at their characters: drink, take dope, perform this or that act of psychological perversion. In good pornography, as in good writing of any kind, the characters need no such external prompting. But Steiner goes on to compare pornographers with S.S. guards, who barked their orders at living men and women:

"The total attitudes are not, I think, entirely distinct. There may be deeper affinities than we as yet understand between the 'total freedom' of the uncensored erotic imagination and the total freedom of the sadist. That these two freedoms have emerged in close historical proximity may not be coincidence."

But have they? History refutes the argument. Sadists were indulging their grisly whims centuries before the modern era of sadistic pornography. Slaughter for fun is not a recent invention. Gilles de Rais was exploiting it to the full long before the Marquis de Sade began his missionary activities; like all enthusiasts of his kind, in whatever period, Gilles needed sadistic books to inflame him about as much as a Madras curry needs a pepper mill.

The question of banning de Sade has been urgently debated in England ever since the Moors Murder trial in

1966, at which a neofascistic Scot named Ian Brady and his mistress, Myra Hindley, were sentenced to life imprisonment for a series of explicitly sadistic killings. Their victims were a seventeen-year-old youth and two children aged ten and twelve. Among the books found in Brady's lodgings was a study of the life and ideas of the Marquis de Sade. Did it supply him with fantasy scenarios which he later enacted in reality? Was this a case of life imitating art? Pamela Hansford Johnson, the novelist and wife of C. P. Snow, suspects that it might have been, and has poured her qualms into an agitated little book called *On Iniquity*. In it she comes out strongly against the free dissemination of pornography. "There is a tyranny of libertarianism as well as of restriction," she says, "and we can already hear its baying, and the rolling of its tumbrils." Miss Hansford Johnson is no professional bigot; she is a decent liberal in a state of sincere unease; but a cool survey of the facts suggests that her natural horror at the Brady-Hindley crimes has carried her to irrational extremes. Brady's record shows that he was cutting up live cats with a flick knife at the age of ten; and around the same time he tied up a school friend and tried to burn him to death. He was a practicing sadist before he ever heard of de Sade.

To my mind, the really evil books about physical cruelty are those which give it a moral justification. I am thinking, for example, of those Catholic tracts that appeared at the bloody high noon of the Inquisition, telling true believers that it was necessary to maim and incinerate unrepentant heretics for the good of their souls. I think, too, of military manuals on the use of bayonets and small arms, which teach you how to inflict the most refined and crippling pain for the greater good of your country. I despise such books and regret that there are people who like to read them. But I would not ban them.

One inalienable right binds all mankind together—

the right of self-abuse. That—and not the abuse of others—is what distinguishes the true lover of pornography. We should encourage him to seek his literary pleasure as and where he finds it. To deny him that privilege is to invade the deepest privacy of all.

*Peter Michaelson*

---

# *HOW TO MAKE THE WORLD SAFE FOR PORNOGRAPHY*

The way to make the world safe for pornography is to show it that sex is good for business. It sounds simpler, however, than it is. It won't do, for example, to say that sex *is* good business, because one becomes, then, a greedy sex-monger. Greed and profit, remember, are not the same. Profit is good; greed is bad. How much profit is equivalent to greed? "If you don't like it here go back to Russia where you came from." Besides, we're enlightened now and we know that sex is bad only when it's *dirty*. How does sex get dirty? "It gets dirty when there's too much of it." How much is . . . ? "Well, you don't have to have your nose rubbed in it to know about it." Couldn't those with sensitive noses decline the gambit? "It would be nice to think that people knew their own noses, but it's not realistic." What has to happen, in short, is that one clean up sex and show that, though it's perfectly businesslike, it isn't tainted by filthy lucre. For however much we may think money is its own reward, we'll not risk its spoliation. Help us, ye gods, to keep money clean.

*Playboy* magazine, perhaps more than any other single pop culture phenomenon, has managed to change sex from a dirty joke into "entertainment served up with humor, sophistication, and spice," to purloin a phrase from its original apology. *Playboy* has been a paradigmatic force in making the world safe for pornography because it has always been careful to use sex for "higher" ends—essentially for the establishment of its fundamental image, the well-heeled Playboy who can and should afford his monthly Playmate. From its beginnings *Playboy* projected the image of a latter-day (executive *né* business) man of mode; again from the credo of its first issue, "We like our apartment. We enjoy mixing up cocktails and an hors d'oeuvre or two, putting a little mood music on the phonograph, and inviting in a female acquaintance for a quiet discussion on Picasso, Nietzsche, jazz, sex." The audience was intended to be, as it has proved to be, "young men-on-the-move" (another *Playboy* PR phrase). It was intended to be and has become a magazine for the young executive, and, more inclusively, for the hopeful fantasies of aspiring pre-executives. But, more than anything else, it is a monumental pop celebration of commodity.

*Playboy* has grown, in fifteen years, from the twice-hocked furniture of its founder Hugh Hefner's apartment to a 54 million dollar "empire," as we are told in the 1968 financial report from *Playboy;* and we are reminded by Hefner—president of the enterprise—that, being a private corporation, *Playboy* is not required to make a public financial statement. He does it, presumably therefore, because he *wants* to. And if there is any question about *Playboy*'s most important product, one need only check its own public relations brochures. The introductory paragraph of one, the cover of which shows the new Playboy Building backed up by Chicago's Gold Coast, goes thus:

> Topped with the world's largest aviation beacon, the Playboy Building at 919 North Michigan Avenue in Chicago is today the headquarters of one of the brightest lights in the world of entertainment for men—*Playboy.* A landmark since its construction, the building, formerly called the Palmolive Building, is a fitting symbol for a magazine and subsidiary enterprises which have witnessed lightning success during the past decade.

One might note here that after *Playboy* moved out of its old Ohio Street buildings it took the United States Post Office and the Museum of Contemporary Art to fill its "shoes." Another blurb, entitled "The Playboy Empire," begins so:

> The $12,000,000 Playboy Club-Hotel at Lake Geneva, Wis., represents one of the most ambitious projects in the history of the Playboy empire. It is the 19th Club in the international chain which includes locations in Atlanta, Baltimore, Boston, Chicago, Cincinnati, Denver, Detroit, Kansas City, Los Angeles, Miami, New Orleans, New York, Phoenix, St. Louis and San Francisco, plus Montreal and London. It is the second Club-Hotel to be operated by Playboy Clubs International, Inc.—the first one debuted in Ocho Rios, Jamaica, in January 1965. Today the Playboy Clubs have some 650,000 keyholders and additional Clubs and Club-Hotels are now being planned for areas including New Jersey, Southern Spain, San Juan and Acapulco.

So Alpha, and so Omega:

> As *Playboy* grew, so did its related enterprises. A Playboy Jazz Festival featuring practically every name jazz artist was held in Chicago in 1959. It was the largest in history, with 68,000 people attending. Hefner conceived and produced *Playboy's Penthouse,* a syndicated latenight television show. A second TV show, *Playboy After Dark,* is now being shown. Playboy Press, the book division, and *VIP,* the magazine for keyholders, were organized. The Playboy Theater, specializing in outstanding U.S. and foreign films, opened in Chicago; Playboy Models was set up; and Playboy Products, marketing apparel and gifts, was initiated.
>
> With the continuous growth of the Playboy empire, plans are now under way for a major expansion into the motion picture and television industries.

Commodity is the beginning and the end.

But profit is really the simplest and even most predictable of *Playboy*'s achievements. More complex and more culturally significant is the cause of that awful success—*Playboy*'s adroit use of sex. So adroit has it been, in fact, that one has the uncomfortable feeling that Richardson's *Pamela*, an old flame of ours, has not done with us yet. One feels, in the image of the Playboy, that Pamela's Squire has been mightily domesticated (and calling domesticity "urbanity" or "sophistication" doesn't relieve the anxiety). Yet again from the original credo: "Most of today's 'magazines for men,' spend all their time out-of-doors —thrashing through thorny thickets or splashing about in fast-flowing streams. We'll be out there too, occasionally, but we don't mind telling you in advance—we plan to spend most of our time inside. We like our apartment." Etc. The rest we've already seen. And not the Playboy's broadest, knowingest wink, not even a desperate psychedelic discussion of Picasso, Nietzsche, jazz, *and* sex all at the same time can dissuade us that Pamela hasn't stuffed that velvet smoking jacket and silk scarf with the carcass of her long tamed Squire, put a high-ball in his hand, a cigarette holder in his teeth, an impressionistic nude on his paneled den wall, and called him PLAYBOY. At last Pamela and the Squire are on equal terms (a fact which *Cosmopolitan* magazine has recently recognized much to its own advantage), and Pamela, our vital parts firmly in her grip, demands, "and now Monsieur your wallet." Hemingway warned us, but we wouldn't listen.

The first thing, then, that *Playboy* has done by equating sex with profit is to sublimate it from its fearful psychic depths to the heights of that "fitting symbol formerly called the Palmolive Building." And, by being made into capital, sex has been psychologically neutralized. It has become a contemporary (and historical) community standard: it has proved profitable and therefore socially redeeming. Concomitant, of course, with *Playboy*'s showing cause for sex has been its cleaning up of the image of sex. Attributing the observation to a Kinsey Institute authority, Nat Lehrman, a senior editor of the magazine, says that *Playboy* has raised sex to respectability, made it fit matter for coffee conversation (along, remember, with Picasso, Nietzsche, and jazz). This is probably true, but in the beginning *Playboy* had some difficulty getting launched into the antiseptic sex imagery which is its latter-day hallmark.

The early foldouts called "Playboy's Eyeful" then, were standard low-grade skin pictures. Nor did they have the now-familiar personality sketch accompanying them. It took three years for the Playmate image to find the girl-next-door quality that now has currency. *Playboy* legend has it that one Janet Pilgrim, a circulation secretary whose name is still on the masthead, went to Hefner requesting a new typewriter. He told her she'd have to pose nude for it, à la Lady Godiva. She did, and the Playmate image was born—bright-eyed, bushy- (I beg your pardon?) tailed, and clean, clean, clean. Up to this time (about 1955), as one editor acknowledges, the magazine was obliged to use either "hookers" or professional models for its foldouts and the image was, excepting perhaps the celebrated Marilyn Monroe calendar nudes featured in the first issue, more sleazy than piquant. And, though Jack Kessie, *Playboy*'s managing editor, claims that the sublimated *Playboy* Image we can now perceive was planned from the magazine's inception, sleaziness pretty much describes its character for at least the first four or five issues. Such photographic features, for example, as "Strip Quiz," a Paris *bistro* strip routine, or Beaux Arts Ball, a portfolio of prurient snapshots, or illustrations of criminal assault, indicate something of the imagistic tone of the first three issues. The fourth issue, though, presented two marvellously prophetic features. One is called "Sex Sells a Shirt," and simply shows a girl taking off her clothes, including of course her shirt. The text, in its banal way, discusses sex and merchandising for a few column inches. It intends to say nothing, and it does. But this nevertheless is the first public presentation of the profit formula on which *Playboy* was to ride to fiscal glory. The other feature is billed as a pictorial history of surgery, and it is essentially a vehicle for naked ladies pictured in the context of medical history. Sex, thus, is both a delight and an instruction, satisfying not only classical poetics but, more importantly, providing the proper scholarly elevation for so base a subject. This kind of augmentation was also to become an editorial staple of the magazine's success formula.

Today's Playmate through which the *Playboy* Image is projected, is the scrupulously antiseptic incarnation of almost virginal contemporary community standards, an occasional lapse into prostitution notwithstanding. And she even has sufficient social redemption potential to be rented out to colleges over football weekends. At which, to show her healthy respect for the Working Man (or Labor or The People or the Dollar—as you prefer), she will charge overtime for conversation above and beyond an eight hour day. (This really happens!) Playmates, lest their title be misleading, do not indulge idle pleasure for its own sake; the meter on these puritanic taxi-dancers is always running. And well it might, for Nathaniel West to the contrary, a clean young girl is always worth more than a clean old man—especially on a college football weekend at an all-male college.

Especially too when one notes that *Playboy*'s notion of its editorial "responsibility" is to serve, according to managing editor Jack Kessie, as a guidebook to the good life for the young, university-educated man. The vocabulary *Playboy* editors use to describe their magazine and its goals reads like Dr. Johnson's own lexicon of aesthetic terms: Balance, Proportion, Taste, Elegance, Imagination, Wit, etc. And it is easily acknowledged that *Playboy is* the most balanced, tasteful, elegant, imaginative, and witty skin book in the business. (By "skin book" I don't of course mean *skin* at all, but rather skin sublimated to *capital.* In which sense one understands that *Playboy* is the more honestly pornographic analogue of *Fortune* magazine. Though it is less honest, and therefore more obscene, than the *Evergreen Review.* So much for the periodical scheme of things.) Of all the terms in the *Playboy* vocabulary, "taste" is perhaps the most significant. "We present sex," says Kessie, "in proportion to its overall degree of importance in man's life." This is true, but it's not the whole truth. In modesty, Kessie ignores the fact that, in making sex a respectable thing and in demonstrating its commodity quotient, *Playboy* expanded the popular horizons for sex's over-all degree of importance in man's life. What he means by *Playboy's* tastefulness is that *visually* there is no more sex showing than there should be.

This is elaborated in Kessie's notion of *Playboy's* editorial contribution to the culture. *Playboy* was, he says, the first to assert not only nudity and sex, but also something else—a rounded view of the good life. He points out, for instance, that if *Playboy* "advocates materialism, so do we advocate other things—civil rights for example." And what, after all, is the end of Taste (not to mention Balance, Proportion, Imagination, and Wit) if not to give a rounded view of the good life? The *Playboy* editors are tastefully aware that "too much" of anything—such as civil rights activism or an eyeful of genitals—is bad for standards, of both business and taste. Thus the Playmate has breasts with glamorized nipples, a groin without pubic hair, vagina, or urinary tract, and a backside without anus. She has feminine shape without female, or for that matter even human, function. She is not made for coitus or procreation or motherhood. She has body without consequence. So when it comes to nakedness (absolute nudity) as distinguished from nudity ("tasteful" nudity, guess whose taste: yes, Pamela's), the "cleanliness" of sex is threatened, and so, therefore, is business. "Our standard has been taste," Kessie says, "and of course there is the risk of legal action. We like to think of ourselves as trend-setters, but here we have, for business and other reasons, to wait for society to know its own mind." So, despite the PR assurance that "It was Hefner's unorthodox belief (a belief he still holds today) that editing a magazine should be a personal matter, that the primary criteria for choosing content should be the editor's own taste and judgment rather than the preferences of a preconceived audience," there *is* in fact a preconceived audience—the young, university-educated man—and the taste of the *Playboy* editors has long since been determined by the sublime cultural marriage of commodity and morality. And *Playboy*, one of the massive offspring of that union, has as much as any other cultural product reaffirmed that its parents are indeed one flesh.

The effect of sentimentalizing materialism, i.e., of giving it the moral value of an ideal, is to transform the natural world into a pop art toy which exists for the Playboy's *well-earned* amusement. After all, he brings home the fatback. (Nor can we, in honesty, be condescending to the *Playboy* Image, for it metaphors all of us, the whole consumer culture on which our egos, economics, and politics depend.) Therefore, all things are seen in the context of *Playboy*'s peculiar ethos of amusement. Women, particularly, are *objets d'art*, created for the Playboy fantasy by the photographer's air brush art and in the Image of *Playboy* by the sketch writer's Playmate-as-home-town-girl fictions. The mere idea of his Playmate menstruating, not to mention the disgusting *fact* of it, is enough to make the Playboy impotent. The Playmate is the Playboy's Beatrice. She does not function, she *is*. Like Shakespeare's Cleopatra, age cannot wither nor custom stale her infinite variety; Like Keats' still unravished bride of quietness, she is forever warm and still to be enjoyed, forever panting and young, far above the stinking breath of human passion, and with *her* we avoid after-sex hangover, that "heart high-sorrowful and cloy'd/ burning forehead, and a parching tongue." The Playmate is not an object of sex. She is an object of art, low art to be sure, but art nonetheless. And who put her on that pedestal and on the mantlepiece of our den? Pamela, we smell a rat.

*Playboy*'s pornography consists in its transformation of women—i.e., female human beings—into Playmates and bunnies, i.e., into erotic art objects designed to titillate the sexual sense and then sublimate it into spending money (in the Playboy Clubs hopefully), or into fantasizing about spending money (in *Playboy* magazine). The greenback dollar, in the *Playboy* ethos (and the *Playboy* ethos is fundamentally the capitalistic ethos), is the sublimated analogue of sperm. Money and the making of it is the masculine symbol in this cultural climate. Spending it therefore is the masculine privilege. It is no accident that the verb *spend* is a common pornographic metaphor for male orgasm. And since, in a capitalistic democracy, money can buy everything, women are, as they have really always been, commodities; and all commodities are available to him who has the power to take them. Thus the power to buy becomes, in the capitalistic ethos, the sign of sexual power. So the world is sexualized, and sex is commercialized, and we have a pornographic image of the world—an idealized, socially lionized, metaphor of prostitution as a way of life. And that, traditionally, is what pornography is—the literature of and about whores and whoring.

But then this process is rather subtle, and one is seldom conscious of himself as the Playboy. Nor does one think of his woman as a whore. And so long as he has Playmates, Bunnies, and their analogues the movie sex stars (who of late have been knocking one another's knockers for the chance to be nude on *Playboy*'s pages) he needn't think of her—if he thinks of her at all, his mind being filled with more enticing fantasies—as such, or as property. She may continue in her time-honored rhetorical role of the sometimes dull, sometimes bright but always slightly irrelevant companion. So it is a curiously lonely bed that Pamela after all has made and in which she must lie. But she is not through yet. Having established her ethos, she labors now to imprint her personality. She has before her, therefore, the task of creating a feminine pornography.

Feminine pornography requires a fantasy structure in which women are invited, as women, to be sexually excited. For the socially redemptive pornography we have been considering this means an alteration of the sex-profit nexus. Theoretically it needs a shift from money and expenditure as an exclusively masculine symbology. Imagistically it involves a transition from the *Playboy* cultural mode to that of the Career Girl. The basic model, still of course, is that of *Playboy*. The emphasis is merely reversed—from male cultural potency to female cultural potency. The women's magazine most perspicacious in recognizing the *Playboy* mode and in exploiting it for its own audience and purposes is the new *Cosmopolitan*. *Cosmopolitan* has only recently tapped in to the pornographic tradition we have been considering. And coming from its own imperial stock, the Hearst syndicate, it is not a pornographic empire builder but is merely capitalizing on the female potential of the ethos *Playboy* has by this time stabilized. And though *Cosmopolitan* has its own cultural significance as a feminist pornographic voice, it isn't consequently as historically instructive or important as *Playboy*.

It emerged from the maze of what William Iverson, in a marvelously witty series of *Playboy* articles—"The Pious Pornographers" (1957 and 1964)—called "the bizarre bulletins on glands, guilt, grief, gynecology, and intercourse which are the peculiar specialty of some of America's most widely read sex books—the women's magazines." His general thesis is that women's magazines offer sentimentalized sexual voyeurism which takes the form of a "sick, sad sex approach to the problem of getting a [man to drop his pants] [or a woman to lift her skirts], so that a million-odd women [can] get a few vicarious kicks from 'playing doctor.'" Here is part of what Iverson calls a "sampler" of prurient ladies' home preoccupations:

> *"That inverted nipple seems better than it was," the doctor told Evelyn Ayres after he had concluded his usual examination. "Have you been pulling it out gently several times, morning and night, the way Mary Ann showed you?"*
>
> *"Yes, Doctor . . ."*
>
> *"I believe I told you that there is a difference of medical opinion as to the best method of toughening the nipples . . ."*
>
> *". . . Your uterus is small and firm. . . . Your breasts show no signs of pregnancy engorgement . . ."*
>
> *. . . This was an atavistic dream of a man and woman alone in a Garden of Eden, perfumed, flecked with butterflies. A red petal fell from the African tulip tree . . .*
>
> *"Oh, Bill," she whispered, half-choking. . . . Then he kissed her. Her lips were like orchids—crumpled, soft, cool, moist. They clung to his. Her arms were around his neck . . .*
>
> *The range of frequency in intercourse for couples of twenty-five to thirty-five is great. A few have intercourse as often as twenty to thirty times a month; others only twice a month. For the majority, the average is two or three times a week . . .*
>
> *"If he has his way, it would be every night. It isn't that I'm a frigid wife, for I am not. Once a week (which is my preference) I respond readily . . ."*
>
> Q. *What about the forceful technique of making love? Do you think that women prefer it?*
>
> A. *Sometimes. Many couples think that variation in sex simply means a different position. Variation can also mean a different psychological attitude. If a man surprises his wife, spontaneously, on a Sunday afternoon, or in a different room*

*of the house, aggressively taking her, this type of approach can make their relationship enormously more erotic . . .*

*"He said I was cold, and I said he was oversexed. Once he even wanted to make love at lunchtime!"*

*"Of course it's awfully hard not to. You both want to so much. Sure, Jim used to get fresh with me now and then, but I'd always handle it by saying 'look at the television' or something. But once I thought, oh, why not? . . ."*

*"The hymen is a thin little membrane, Phyllis, stretched across the lower end of the vagina . . ."*

*"Am I afraid to use mine?" I said.*

*"No," George said, "like I say, you're naturally lascivious. You use your pelvis. . . ."*

*I did a little bump.*

*"But I wouldn't go too far," George said. I could feel from his neck that he was beginning to color.*

*"Why do men want sex to be like a burlesque show? Why can't they realize that it is a solemn thing?"*

*". . . And . . . well, one night I drank a can of beer in the car with him, and it happened again . . . I just couldn't help it. After all, girls want it just as much as boys do, don't they?"*

The summing up, where Iverson recalls,

> *the curious saga of Evelyn Ayres, troubled heroine of another stirring episode of 'Tell Me, Doctor,' the* Ladies' Home Journal's *long-playing feature on clinical sex and gynecological horrors. Years of familiarity with its format of fear, disaster and medical salvation had led me to think of this everexpanding anthology of female malfunctions as a kind of crypto-prurient* Memoirs of a Woman of Misery, *in which Evelyn Ayers now starred as the anxiety-fraught Fanny Hill of Breast Feeding.*

There is here a latter-day version of that same morbid sentimentalizing of the faithful servant woman (not Moll Flanders but Pamela) as she resists the forces of aristocratic evil and guile that Richardson exploited for his social class in the eighteenth century. The heroine is essentially the same, but with her social and even economic success in molding the Squire into the Playboy, the nature of the villain has transformed itself to neurosis, obstetrics and gynecology, things unheard-of in Richardson's day. That, if you are not too particular, is progress. But, being an extension of the long-familiar soap opera, it is pretty much predictable. And so one suspects that Iverson's anxiety (*Playboy*'s anxiety) is crowding his condescending wit.

For his real complaint, *Playboy*'s complaint, is not that the women's magazines are *pornographic* (he and *Playboy* know all about that, although such language makes them nervous, being bad for business), it is that they are *obscene.* Nor is his objection to their piety (i.e., sentimentality); he and *Playboy* know all about that too, as we have seen. The problem is that these magazines undermine the Playmate image. Think of the Playmate. Imagine her with inverted nipples! Or menstruating! Or, worse still, imagine her being sexually unsatisfied *after* a bout with the prodigiously phallic Playboy! Smearing her neuroses, obstetrics, and gynecology all over the hard-earned sanctuary of his den. Not only that, as if it weren't enough, they also undermine the *Playboy* Image. Iverson's citation of the following rebuke of vestigial "19th Century Puritanism" is revealing in this regard:

> *All shapes and varieties of marital anguish were laid squarely at the door of the clumsy husband. It was the man, the marriage manuals unanimously declared, who was responsible for success in sex, and equally responsible for its failure. For the enlightened readers of the manuals, making love became a kind of challenge . . .*
>
> *Frequently couples spent so much time worrying about whether their technique was right, whether their climaxes occurred simultaneously as the book said they should, whether the wife really had an orgasm, that they lost all*

*the meaning of marital intercourse, not to mention the pleasure . . .*

*'Pleasure' was a word that the ladies' books had seldom mentioned in connection with sex, and T. F. James' reference to it came as a welcome surprise.*

Iverson argues, though with more clever outrage than analytical energy, for a "recognition of the need for greater sexual responsibility in women . . . (to) reduce the impossible number of restrictions . . . imposed upon the sexual deportment of the American male." The *Playboy* spokesman is annoyed that women, too, want some fun but aren't getting it and are imposing their frustrations on his fantasies. Women, alas, want to *feel* something down there and, alack and alas, they want to feel it more often than men want to make them feel it. *Playboy* may or may not acknowledge the problem. That isn't clear either from Iverson's articles or from *Playboy* generally. What is clear, however, is that *if* there is a problem it is a problem for *women,* so *Playboy* lays it discreetly at their door and strides manfully off to a rendezvous with mood music on the hi-fi and a quiet discussion of Picasso, Nietzsche, jazz, and (still undaunted) sex.

## *Philip Nobile*

---

# *INSIDE* SCREW

Happily, Pitirim Sorokin did not live to see *Tits and Ass, Bang, Desire, Ecstasy, Adults Only, Pussycat, Voyeur, Luv, Fun, Pleasure, Kiss, Cocksure* or *Screw*. Even though these New York City sex tabloids clinically demonstrate his theory of the total disintegration of Western sensate culture, most likely he was unready for such an execrable decline and fall. For eye has not seen, nor ear heard, nor has it entered the heart of the average heterosexual what, for example, Al Goldstein and Jim Buckley have prepared for him in *Screw*.

Justly self-advertised as the "first and best in the field it created," *Screw* sprang full-grown in November, 1968, from the thigh of the blood and lust school of journalism where virgins continually have babies and fathers commonly eat sons.

"I used to do stories about short-cock guys for *Hush-Hush*," confesses executive editor Goldstein, an obese, cheeky reincarnation of the young Everett Sloan. "I once wrote that horse transplants would add inches to a man's enjoyment. I really didn't think anyone would believe it. I thought it was campy. But when the letters came in begging for information, I felt guilty."

Now all shame is gone. Cleansed by his new occupation, Goldstein says, straightfaced, "*Screw* is the right place at the right time." And leave us mention, for the right money. A fluctuating circulation of 98,000 at fifty cents a copy is not a bad weekly haul. Add to that the investment and return on *Screw* T-shirts and posters, a homosexual offshoot entitled *Gay,* a non-verbal *Screw* called *X* to keep the functionally-illiterate opposition honest, an erotic film festival, and an exploitation movie spoofing the marriage manual flicks, and you get an idea of the house that only balls have built. "In the sex field you can be totally stupid and still make money," according to Goldstein, a theory of no presently known refutation.

Filthy lucre goes only so far. Even pornographers worry about the work that lives after them. Putting us on, in part, Goldstein swears, "*Screw* is more important to me than screwing. I get depressed when we do a bad issue. The last time it happened I couldn't talk to Jim for two days.

"Hey, Jim," he shouts across their joint office to his twenty-five-year-old partner, "remember when we put out those bad issues and couldn't talk to each other for two days?" Buckley nods. "See?" Goldstein comes back, reassured in his vocation.

What manner of paper is this that calls forth such sentiment? You have to be there. To tell you that *Screw* covers the waterfront of low-tide erotica with kinky consumer reports, dirty movie ratings, "fuckbook" reviews, scatological cartoons, genital contests and other unspeakable diversions—all packaged between photographs of the most private human parts—conveys little. Until you have fingered through its pages and put your fist into its centerfold, you will not believe. *Screw* is a nasty leap forward for the erogenous zone, unlike anything before, but the vanguard of what is to come in the Scandinaviazation of American sex.

The pornography in *Screw* and its reasonable facsimiles is of the flaccid rather than hard-core Danish kind. Otherwise newsstand sales would be banned. When particular issues are busted, seven of fifty-five heretofore with *Screw,* the vice squad never specifies which picture or illustration went irredeemably beyond the law. Without strict constructionist guidelines, editors must casuistically decide what the community standards can stand. It goes without saying that the act of intercourse cannot be graphically represented. The tumescent male, either alone or with others, is also out of the question. More leeway is allowed to intimations of polymorphous perversity, but it is the better part of discretion to avoid locking loins, hands on nipples and hints of self-abuse.

In the old days, before criminal obscenity charges fouled up the system, *Screw* invented cheery Rube Goldberg combinations of group flesh doing what comes unnaturally and delighted in pranks similar to pasting headshots of John Lindsay and Robert Wagner onto naked torsos (cf. "Getting Into Gracie: A Pussy-Eye View of the Mayoralty Candidates"). But thirty-five thousand dollars for legal defense costs have diminished *Screw*'s bumptious ardor of late. The company lawyer must now pass on all visuals lest any untimely editorial *praecox* spoil the cost-sheets of liberation. Still, John Lennon's fellatious and cunnilingual lithographs, which deliberately trespass against prevailing norms, were printed without harassment. Uncanny. And to this very day, Ralph Ginzburg roams around free.

Who reads *Screw?* One is almost afraid to ask. A half million people, that's who. "Not to like *Screw* is not to be alive in the seventies," suggests editor Buckley, a small fellow with a large phallus (you recognize this immediately from the blue lucite cast of his organ, modestly erected, on his desk). "*Screw* isn't a jerk-off paper," he insists. "When we have a story on how to give a blow-job, it's a sociological statement." *Screw* people are different from you and me. They have more sociology.

The corporate symbol of *Screw* is a cutout of the male groin. "Meat, Our Founding Member," as the totem is named, appears in the disguise of a human face—funny eyeglasses, with bulging Groucho pupils, resting on the penis and a pipe emanating from the side of the hanging scrotum. The gag is on us, of course. “Meat” does not actually exist. He is only a fixation, and though we might manfully wish it, not wholly owned by *Screw.*

*Jeremy Bugler*

---

# *THE SEX SELL*

Once upon a time, the very first love of the advertising man was the eyestopper. Given a tiresome problem, like how to sell a carpet underlay or an industrial glue or a motorcar, the adman called for the eyestopper. Usually, he required it in its most famous form—sex and its symbols. Lying on the carpet, embracing the tube of glue, or sitting on the bonnet, he put the blonde girl with the big boobs and the lacquered-on smile.

Even today you can see, particularly in the trade press, ads that are built only on the eyestopper (which is advertising slang for a device to catch the attention). A current ad in the German *Time*-style magazine, *Der Speigel,* depicts a Nordic girl holding a paper sack; the punchline talks of keeping all the women happy *"mit Müllsäcken aus Kraftpapier"*—with strong paper refuse bags.

But the golden age of the sexual eyestopper, the time when literally any product ad could well feature a girl, has faded. Today sex in British advertising is used with more restriction, but with more intensity. The use is more restricted in that most sexy ads are selling products related to the female body. It is more intense in that sex is not used as a stage prop, but as an integral part of the plot, appealing to sexual fantasy in women. This is why if you want to see fruity ads, you'll find them, overwhelmingly, in the women's magazines—in *Vogue* and *She* and *Honey* and so on.

The decline of the sexual eyestopper, the rise of the

sexual fantasy, has caused a great shift in emphasis in sex in advertising. The place of sex in the market place is today much less widespread than is generally believed. The received opinion—that explicit sex has been pushed right into the forward line, so that modern industrial man can pursue his most important economic activity (to wit, consuming)—is true only in areas that affect intimately modern industrial *woman.*

You can prove the limited use of sex in ads by looking at what were the top advertised product groups last year. According to figures from Legion Publishing Company of England, chocolate confectionery was the most heavily advertised product—27.4 million dollars spent. Very few sweets are sold by sex, except some kinds of after dinner mints and theater chocolates. Mostly, chocolate confectionery ads refer to the food value—"A Mars a day helps you work, rest and play." And while Cadbury's Flake is popularly said to be advertised by a campaign depicting fellatio, the agency concerned firmly denies the charge.

Second to chocolate comes cigarette ads, at 23 million dollars. There's almost no sex here, partly because it's banned now by the Code of Advertising Practice, partly because the companies find pack-and-background ads, without people, most effective. Third come household soaps and detergents at 17.8 million dollars. Again no sex —unless you think that Alan Freeman, the disc jockey who promotes Omo, counts as a sexual device. Next is departmental and chain store advertising—16.8 million dollars. I'd say the sex here would be only where the store is advertising a kind of stocking or corset, or perhaps shirts for men. Fifth is pet food advertising—once more, no sex.

Of the remaining fifteen top advertised product groups, the bulk obviously don't sell on explicit sex—for example, unit trusts (nineteenth), banks (sixteenth), fruit and vegetable (sixth), soups and meat extracts (fourteenth). Some explicit sexual references, though, are made in cigar advertising (twentieth), in quite a number of air travel and transport ads (eighteenth), and sometimes in beer (eighth)—most lagers sell on blondes—and wines (twelfth). An El Cid sherry ad uses a blonde concealing nipple behind bottle.

Of course, it's not hard to think of some ad campaigns which do use sex and yet are not specifically aimed at women. Gas companies are inclined to, partly because they feel the public knows all gases are much alike and that therefore the best way to sell them is not on "mileage capacity" (like Shell) but on an aura. Hence National Benzole's new campaign, which has a couple indulge in mild sex play whilst driving down the road. Regent played the same gambit in the past, with their "Ride Regent" campaign. These ads showed a wild west, be-stetsoned, tight-T-shirted pump girl employing the petrol pump in a somewhat obscene manner. (Perhaps the success of the campaign can be judged by the fact that Regent has decided to change its name to Texaco.)

But, by and large, the great bulk of advertising does not hit us below the belt, in the sense of working on our sexual urges. This is why an advertising man like Winston Fletcher, a director of Waddicors and Clark Wilkinson, maintains that "of all the media, advertising has the least sex." With the exception of music, I'd say he's right. In films, there are the semi-blue films (*The Sweet Sins of Sexy Susan*), the British dirty-joke films (the *Carry On* saga), as well as movies like Pasolini's *Teorama,* which shows the private parts of Terence Stamp in clear outline through his trousers. And sex abounds in books and on stage.

Good reasons exist for this relative puritan performance (in terms of sex) by advertising. As Winston Fletcher says, for one thing the larger firms and corporations shun it. As ad campaigns get doctored by innumerable company committees, sex tends to get censored. For another thing, and more important, sex is irrelevant to most products, because, to quote Winston Fletcher: "It is hard to convince the public that your product alone has a monopoly of sexiness. I mean, you might convince me that cigar sucking is sexy, but you won't convince me that Castella only will give me this sexy feeling."

The whole theory of advertising today, says Fletcher, is that "it must be more or less believable" on one plane or another. To try to sell carpet cleaner, say, on sex is just incredible. What sexy advertising there is, he says, comes mainly from small agencies with small clients, and he explains the number of ads that feature nudes with "admen and a certain type of advertiser enjoy nude photographic sessions."

This is exaggeration if only because otherwise the agencies hawking cosmetics and underwear accounts would have a monopoly of the advertising industry's voyeurs. For it is principally the cosmetic and underwear products that capitalize on explicit sex in their advertisements. Combined with an uncensored editorial line in the actual text of the magazines they have made the women's fashion magazines second only to the "men's magazines"—*Playboy, Penthouse,* and the rest—on a nipple count. Thus a recent issue of *She* has eleven nudes shown, five of them in ads.

This phenomenon started with a Colman Prentis and Varley campaign in 1960 for the Unilever soap called Breeze. According to John Pearson and Graham Turner, in their book *The Persuasion Industry* (Eyre and Spottiswoode, 1965), the agency wanted "to try to get across in advertising the actual sensual pleasure a woman gets in using soap." To do this, the agency used a nude model, actually wearing soap. The result was the first nipples-and-all nude in British advertising (in the *Daily Mirror,* this ad had the nipples blocked out).

Today, the Breeze ad is entirely unexceptional. In

thinking, its heir is a current campaign put out by Crawfords Advertising for British Enkalon. The product is a type of a yarn used in stocking manufacture, brand-named Enkasheer, and claimed to be softer than most. Crawfords decided on a nude presentation that is more explicit than any yet. The Enkalon account executive, Ian McLaren says: "We are not trying to say to readers—if you wear stockings with Enkasheer, you'll get laid. And we didn't put in nipples just to get attention. It was a matter of identification—we wanted to try to put the reader in the position where she's actually enjoying the sensation of putting on her stockings." Hence the punch-line: "A new sensation from British Enkalon."

But the nudity also sprang from a technical point: how do you show tights on a woman's body without also showing her naked, or wearing an improbable upper garment? Sweaters come down too far, apparently; as McLaren says: "Years ago, the ads finished at the thigh, but then so did the stockings."

The problem of illustrating the product was also a key factor in an ad the Havas agency did for a Fabergé perfume, Aphrodisia. This ad, in my opinion, goes farther than two dozen stocking nudes put together. The problem that faced John Hovington and John Bainbridge of Havas was that they wanted to show the perfume actually being used. They wanted to sell on Fabergé's strong points: the very exotic packs and the novel method it embodies of putting on the perfume—on the ball-point principle.

Hovington says: "We had a choice of places to show it being applied. A girl puts perfume on behind her ears between her breasts, on her wrists, on the inside of her elbow and the inside of her knee. . . . We wanted to underline that Fabergé is unusual and a bit adventurous, so we didn't want the most conventional place. We rejected the place between the breasts as being too blatant and in the end we prefered behind the knee as the use of it in this place isn't as well known in Britain as in the U.S. or France."

The decision to use a huge close-up of the phallic-like applicator being inserted into the wedge between calf and thigh was thus partly dictated. "We wanted great big close-ups of the perfume being applied—not just the package or just the woman like other ads." The sexy effect is heightened by the copy line "Aphrodisia says what most perfumes daren't even whisper," and the clever base-line, "Fabergé—a fragrant breach of the rules," written by copywriter Gail Amber. As for the phallic symbol, Hovington says: "This was accidental, in that the package came first. We didn't deliberately say—we must get a phallic symbol. But when it evolved, we didn't mind."

The Fabergé ad gets its effect not least because it fails to show the whole female body. Charles Rycroft, speaking as a psychoanalyst, considers the ad obscene insofar as it fragments the body. "It depersonalises the body; it's on the same principle that a woman who's half undressed is more erotic than one who is naked."

Indeed, in Rycroft's view, one of the basic appeals of the sexy stockings-cosmetic-swimsuits ads is to "the way women often look on themselves as sexual objects." This makes a convincing explanation of the phenomenon of the nude ads.

Rycroft's point is born out particularly by the Nelbarden swimwear campaign, which is probably the most remarked-upon poster campaign the London Underground has ever carried. The posters are explicitly come-hitherish; they feature girls in aggessive or alluring sexual postures—complete with protuberant *mons veneris* and legs far enough apart to drive a truck through.

Deliberately, nearly all the photographs for the posters are shot from a low angle, looking up to the crotch. They have phallic symbols—swords, oars, masts—intentionally included. Great care is taken with the mood of the photography; the models are all photographed in continental resorts so that they get a good, rather than English, tan. Their swimsuits, if necessary, are padded to bulge voluptuously. Certain Nelbarden swimsuits are even marketed *just because* they'll look voluptuous on an Underground poster—for example, a 1968 creation that looked like a baby's diaper, with a large pin. (It made its model, Marilyn Rickard, a kind of mini-celebrity.)

The campaign has been running for seven years, getting more explicit with each passing year. During this time, Nelbarden has grown from a minor to major swimwear manufacturer. It would appear that posters with a direct, blatant sexual appeal to men have induced women to go out and buy. The campaign's creator, Tony Leniston, explains the success by saying: "I wanted to sell an idea, a romance." He says: "A large proportion of the women who buy Nelbarden swimwear are in their late twenties, early thirties. They have bulging tummies, operation scars—they've had a couple of kids. . . . This is why Nelbarden bikinis, in fact, are not brief. They wouldn't cover up enough."

Leniston goes on: "So I wanted to create this aura of glamour, excitement, sex. I wanted a mood of escapism, to appeal to a woman so she feels that if she buys a Nelbarden swimsuit, she'll find herself in a situation of sun and romance—even if she never gets farther than Brighton."

Rycroft says of the ads: "Sometimes when women are depressed they go out and buy something. This is the same idea—that you can attach to yourself a symbol which will alter your mental state." He comments also that the ads make a kind of sexual appeal that would not, sexually, arouse women, the people at whom the ads are aimed: "This is the most interesting part . . . it seems to involve this tendency of women to conceive of themselves as objects . . . and also the idea a woman may have that if she's not being looked at, she's not real."

If the motivation *is* the tendency of women to conceive of themselves as objects, it explains well why sex in ads is nearly always sex in a cosmetics or an underwear ad, or a clothing ad. As a thesis, it is supported by other examples. One is an ad for Triumph underclothing, which depicts a girl in underwear being paraded before an Arabian sheik and his henchmen. The sheik is considering whether to buy her. (The copy reads: "Undies to be sold in. . . . The will of Allah could catch you in your undies at any time. Blushmaking? Not in Triumph fashion undies.") It is completely concerned with the fantasy of the girl-as-sexual-object.

A second supporting example is the poster campaign for Elliott boots, put out by Dunn-Meynell, Keefe. The posters use nude non-European models. The creative director of the agency, Bob Wright, wrote in the trade magazine, *Campaign:* "What we do when we show a nude girl is to offer the ultimate in being daring and then allow the girl who buys and wears the boots the opportunity to be seen by other people as the daring girl in the poster. In fact, she can create her own fantasy by degrees. The extreme would be the feeling that she is also nude wearing just boots. More likely, she wants to feel that others *think* she is as daring as that." Once more, in short, the element of passivity, of being perceived by others, allied to fantasy.

The Elliott campaign is also worth remarking because it obeys a rule about sex in ads, which says: be sexy, but not too much. (The Nelbarden posters are an exception in this perhaps because the beach is an arena of extravert sexual display.) Bob Wright thus says of the Elliott posters: "There must be a safety valve. Note the arrogance with which a mini-skirt is worn. Why? Because the companion fashion to wear tights is the safety factor. Blatant sexuality tempered with clinical purity. When we present a nude wearing boots, we can see our target audience satisfying its desire to exhibit itself through the safety of the fantasy situation. This is even further reinforced in terms of safety by the use of a non-European model . . ."

Exactly the same trait can be found in a current campaign for Badedas, the bath "additive." The ads, by the Allen Brady and Marsh agency, depict two situations: one a girl in a bath towel looking out of a window at the arrival of a handsome man, who has arrived with Rolls Royce and Chinese chauffeur. The other shows a man in a bath towel, looking at a girl, who just stepped down from a helicopter. (Both situations were necessary as Badedas sells to men and women.) The campaigns were chosen to combine "the fantasy of the sexual promise and the realism of the bath," to quote *Campaign.*

In the same article, the director of the agency, is quoted on why it was decided to have the girl descending from a helicopter: "It was difficult to find the type of girl who comes around for a man. Having her get out of a helicopter is okay because it's improbable. Otherwise you'd simply have a woman hunting for a man, which people don't like."

Thus, both the Elliott and Badedas campaigns illustrate the principle of some sex, but not too much. Both campaigns walk a knife edge between realism and fantasy; both are very careful not to be blatantly exciting. Too overt an effect would produce a kind of commercial pornography which would destroy any chance of the woman being able to relate to the ad and to hitch herself to the fantasy.

This is why there's a chasm between the type of nudes in the fashion magazines and the girl-of-the-month exhibits in the *Playboy*-type periodical. It's also relevant to the fact that sexy ads fail to convince when they aren't related to products concerned with the female sexual persona. Sex is a very bad way of selling *Müllsäcken aus Kraftpapier.* It's quite a good way, though, of selling sex.

## *Robert Craft*

---

# *PAYDIRT:*
# *NOTES*
# *ON THE SEX EXPLOSION*

## *I. Hollywood*

> "A copy of Michelangelo's David is being displayed at Forest Lawn Memorial Park here without a figleaf. 'We thought the time had come to try it,' said Charles Pink, manager."
>
> —*New York Times,* 7/20/69

Lunch at The Telephone Booth is no ordinary "feed," though the point is not food, of course, but rather the topless and bottomless waitresses who serve it and take turns "dancing" on a dais. The ringside seats for these ballets are at the bar, but the performers' charms, both fore and aft, are in direct or mirror view of every table. The room is dark, the more fulgently to set off powdered and spotlighted epidermises, and at the same time shield the viewers, some of whom, as if expecting a televised police raid, hide behind smoked glasses as well.

Who *are* the viewers? Leering lechers? Inveterate voyeurs? Not all of them, at any rate; a bashful gastronome in the booth next to mine hardly bothers to glance in the direction of the dais, or for that matter away from his plate. As for the overt and steady watchers, most of them seem to share a predilection for bosoms, seldom lowering their sights from that level, at all events, though a more bizarre penchant, if it existed, would be unobservable in the circumstances anyway.

The girls wear short black jackets during their stints of waiting on tables (i.e., pushing drinks). These are shed on the dais—where each dancer is cued by her "own" recording (her favorite? the only one she recognizes?)—but they conceal so little in the first place that the strip is teaseless. All the same, the first disrobing provokes an exclamation—"Get a load of that!"—from an ogler newly installed at the bar. "That" is a case of bouncy overendowment which the girl seems to defy the customers to notice, looking them straight in the eyes, if that is where *they* are looking. But her ballet is a dilly, and really indescribable unless it might be called pussyfooting.

A platinum *Esquire*-cartoon blonde appears next, wearing pasted-on, stage-prop tits, very sheer panty-hose (against the chill? to conceal some foam-rubber supplementation?), and a *moue*. She is half bombed, I think, but her dance, no bacchanal, might have been mimicked from a circus pooch. She cannot be more than twenty-three, which is middle-aged in this profession, yet she is repelled by sex, obviously, and contemptuous of men. At what more halcyon time of life did she discover that her "virtue" was irretrievable, I wonder, and how many more years as an itinerant go-go stripper, graduating to call-girl, will she be able to take before losing the last few of her marbles and being carried off with the screaming meemies?

The next girl is, at the other extreme, tough, able to take care not only of herself but of every man in the room, some of whom may have been taken care of already, in fact, judging by her claque. Apart from a Theseus-like wish concerning the thin gold chain of her G-string, however, I am not inspired by any lewd ambition at all which, alas, could be a sign of Craft ebbing. She is too angular for Ingres (*Le Bain Turc*) and would not have fetched the top price in a seraglio, but at the same time has a localized tendency, perhaps from usage, to sag and to pleat. But while the other girls do no more than go through their paces barely, she puts soul into hers, simulating the throes of the denouement with egregious thrusts and excruciating gyrations. "Hey, that hurts," one castration-threatened spectator cries out, and another, evidently still more worried, rounds on him with: "It would break it off." At this point a dirty old man at the bar chimes in with "How'd ya like to take *her* home?" the answer to which—"Yeah, only anywhere but there"—probably comes from a married man. Strutting off after her number, the nymph confesses that "these Monday mornings are really getting to me," but a suggestion is offered from the floor for this, too: "Why don't you go and entertain our troops in Sweden?"

The next girl, tall, Junoesque, dallying long hair (a postiche?) down her back from a bandeau, is the beauty of the bevy—sculpturally considered, at least—but her movements are muzzy (from smoking "grass"? oncoming menses?). She is the only one, in any case—that cadent, if rented hair—who could raise my libidinal temperature a therm, but then, only a necrophiliac could be seriously bothered by the other exposures. After her "act" I tell her that, of all the girls, she would look the best in clothes (well, see-through and cellophane clothes, anyway), but she is not certain that the remark is entirely complimentary, and her smile turns to a "level-with-me-Mister" expression. She is the least at home here of all the girls, at any rate, and that in itself goes a long way toward making her the most attractive. Her name is Christine (she says). If I were to call her that another time, she would probably look at me "hard," trying to remember when we had slept together.

The "kicks" from non-haptic sex, the sexual object under a glass bell—not the *girls'* "kicks," which apart from the money appear to be related to the child's wish to discard its clothes and be noticed—depend in part on the satisfaction of aesthetic criteria, which in turn are governed by the subject's psychological make-up as a whole. Attempts to isolate and measure male susceptibilities to female form, qua form, are now being made, in fact, simply by projecting adjustable outlines of female shapes on a screen, and enlarging, shrinking, and otherwise modifying them to the subjects' desiderations. The latter are both avowed and, because of the unreliability of imputing the exact tendency of the attraction to the impulse, determined by electrical sensing devices. So far, after co-ordination with other personality data, the findings indicate that breast-fixated college-age American males are better adjusted than bottom-fixated ones; and that options favoring comparatively large amplitudes—a rise in the graph—earn correspondingly higher psycho-social stability marks.

In the absence of co-ordination between the natural and social sciences, however, this does not appear to be a pragmatically conclusive fact, while in view of the present low opinion of physiological testing of this kind generally, one may even doubt that it is a fact at all. (The retardation of the heartbeats and consequent conservation of oxygen in submerging crocodiles was thought until lately to be one of all-wise Nature's protective devices, but it has now been discovered that the slow-downs are caused entirely by fear of the scientific experimenters! See *Nature*, 7/12/69.) Further research along these (adjustable) lines will undoubtedly continue, nevertheless, as sex is further removed, and finally entirely separated from procreation.

Meanwhile, it is certainly better to "make love, not war." (And no matter that the biological overlove in love-making is as wasteful as overkill: a mere seventeen nuclear missiles are said to be enough to destroy human life on the planet, but thousands already exist, so, too, a single sperm cell is enough to create human life, yet each ejaculation of male seed contains at least two hundred and fifty million of them. Did you ever think of that, Mr. Portnoy?) Necessary as it was, however, and whatever, if anything, it may have had to do with love, the sex explosion—as distinct from a long-awaited and more profoundly subversive Revolution of Eros—has become a bore. One already looks forward to a time beyond it when it will be possible to do it and forget about it and even go on to other things. "We liberate sexuality not in order that men may be dominated by [it]," Freud wrote (in 1908!), "but in order to make a suppression possible." *Voilà!* Temptation exists to be resisted.

## *II. New York*

The first half-hour of *Skin,* said to be representative of the new sex flicks, takes place at the Botanical Gardens—in order to compare the phalli of humans and flora, it would seem, except that the former never appear, and one begins to suspect that the title really refers to lemons or oranges. The dermatological mystery deepens in the next scene, which is about drug-taking and the Bay Area needle set, but in the scene after that a derrière (just the rondures, no connecting anatomy!) canters about the screen in time with the D-minor organ fugue from *Fantasia.* What was it Plato said about "the desire and pursuit of the whole"?

* * *

Television commercials here are beginning to exploit the third-sex market. "For women only," says a lesbian contralto on behalf of "Virginia Slims," which are being promoted as a Sapphic cigarette. And an advertisement for an electric lawnmower, after demonstrating the machine's superiority over a grazing sheep, considers whether the animal might be made a meal of, but concludes that "that would be like eating the gardener." The next thing you know, says I.S., homosexuals will be demanding equal time.

*Oh! Calcutta!*, on the other hand, is for regular guys. Or *is* it? Are the men the real attraction, perhaps, and the women merely decoys? Men in pairs—fissiparous sex—account for a large part of the audience, in any case, though most of the episodes deal with country matters and none, I think, is construable, except wholly transposed, as their "scene." But whatever the audience's sectarian proclivities—and the other conspicuous feature is the absence of the young and the freaked-out—it inhibits as an entity. Communality on such a scale at a peep show contradicts ancient, if anti-social, notions of privacy. Nor does one's consciousness of the communality ever let up, thanks to the univocal laughter, embarrassed at first, perhaps, but first, last, and most other times embarrassing.

Anthropologists are currently explaining the limitation of pornography to male fantasies as a consequence of the involvement of "more extensive higher cortical control" in male sexual activity than in female. However that may be, sexual functionalism, together with the decline, for other reasons as well, of the mystery of sexuality, is challenging the taken-for-granted supremacy of the female nude, as well as the bartering-bride system which obliges or encourages women to think of their bodies—and men to think of women's bodies—as their most valuable possession; which can't be a very welcome development to the woman in the street.

But the male nude on stage is handicapped (if that is the word for it) by the veto against virile members—not in dramas involving urological examinations, of course, but certainly in amorous action pieces à la *Calcutta*. A young man in the buff, mounting a young and comely woman in the same, is expected, in time, to register a visible physical reaction. But the young man in *Calcutta* remains sapless and detumescent, and whatever the reason —saltpeter? pederasty? sexual shell-shock? androgen deficiency? the milking of the actors, like vipers, before each performance?—his failure to become potent does not consort with the minimum realistic requirement of the circumstances.

While no holds are barred on stage, it seems that erections are countenanced only in films, some of the latest of which, whether or not for that reason, have become pilot courses in the phenomenon. And this double standard not only denies the stage actor full expression, but exposes him to prejudicial reflections on his abilities, and even on his character, implying, as it does, that he must behave like "a thief in the night," if he behaves at all, and thus is to be relegated to the same class of invertebrates (morally speaking) as Blake's worm. The double standard becomes triple, quadruple, quintuple, moreover, when compounded with bookselling laws, actual sex laws (different in every state), and the Blue Laws of the Independent Government of Television whose theater critics, incidentally, would be unable even to describe *Calcutta* with apt and ultimate brevity, the word being banned on the "medium."

Nudity wears off quickly. In fact *clothes* are not long off in *Calcutta*—but long enough for the observation of details satisfying on the whole, it seems, to male egos—before the audience is ready (at least) to receive an entirely new cast of bodies (well, you would hardly call it a *dramatis personae*). But the interchangeability of bodies, and the greater uniformity in nude than clothed ones, are premises of the depersonalizing treatment of sex—the only possible treatment, I should add, if the third-party role of the audience is not to be intolerable.

A further premise is that starting over again with clothes can reinvigorate. It is so to some extent in the sado-masochistic fantasy scene, where a fully-clothed girl carrying a rod, kneels head to floor, bottom high and audienceward, and one by one, but forestalling the final one, upraises her numerous petticoats. The raising of the final one is a foudroyant effect (comparatively)—abetted by a good countdown technique—the sheer effrontery (or backery) of which, until dissipated by overexposure, seems to hold the audience in a euphoric trance. An unrelated-to-other-features bottom loses identity, however, and *we* lose our bearings, soon forgetting what it is—an enlarged peach? an *idée fixe?*—and why we are basking in it. Finally, too, we are disappointed not to witness even one piquant tap with that rod, for *her* sake, if she really likes it.

On balance, *Calcutta* is probably worth the while, for purely negative reasons, of anyone anxious to see standards of "erotic culture" improved. And in that sense its most sizable service is simply in obviating further, future demonstrations of how dull sex can be as a subject for a full evening—yet *is* not that necessarily or *sui generis;* but *Calcutta* neglects the variety of the subject; it might, for instance, and to advantage, have interspersed the bedwork scenes with illustrations of the "polymorphous perverse," peeking at selected fetishes, or better, bestiality, for that would at least allow for some horseplay.

The undesirabless of puerility even in pornography is fully, positively demonstrated as well, most unfortunately (for *Calcutta*) in the two episodes which had starting possibilities as social satire, the take-off on "swinging" via the sex want-ad columns, and the send-up of the Masters and Johnson sex institute. The latter is the most nearly successful caper of the evening, nevertheless, partly because the clinical view of sex exactly fits the case, and partly because the tables are turned to show that the "sexual response" of the volunteer lovers—who are attached with electrodes and wired to a computer-like console that lights up when intercourse begins—is far less remarkable than that of the kinky institute staff.

What, I wonder, not breathlessly, will be the role of the "artistic merit" and "redeeming social value" clauses when the moribund "living theater" moves on from group therapy to the theater of intercourse, and when actors and actresses break with the convention of laying each other onstage and come down and lay the audience? At the present rate of escalation, by which onstage erections may well be *de rigueur* in another six months, and in a year or so *Calcutta* itself could be making a comeback as camp, the possibility is not far away. (Does anyone still recall that only two years ago the Mayor himself had to overrule a ban on some bare-breasted African *danseuses*, and that he could do so only because they were savages, after all, and it didn't matter?) My own prediction is that *Calcutta* will be regarded by historians of the subject as a large step in the betrayal of the sexual revolution, betrayal through conformism.

I wonder, too, whether *Calcutta* celebrates sexual freedom as much as it does sexual frustration. Catharsis in any sense at all—let alone well, what *was* that "function" old Wilhelm Reich once made so much of?—has never seemed more remote. "I want it now," moans a singer at the end, but *does* anyone?—do even sexual have-nots?—as a result, that is, of incitement by these exhibitions? Or are the latter something of an anti-arouser, in the sense that while substitute performances may nourish the sexual imagination, can they not also reduce it, by invasions not so much of physical as of mental privacy?

Myself, I am beginning to think that the unclothed state may have been intended only for the gods—and *chez eux:* even sea-changed Venus was draped before her entry into the mortal sphere, after all—or for those who, like the Doukhobors and the Digambara, practice it in the names of gods. But that is to forget two other passages suitable for the condition: "Naked I came into the world, naked I shall go."

*Ross Wetzsteon*

---

# STAGED SEXUALITY

We've all known that sexual intercourse on stage was coming soon—the only question, really, was would anyone beat Kenneth Tynan to it? (In fact, at the current rate of escalation, I'd found myself hoping my baby daughter wouldn't want to go out for her junior high school play—which will probably have allegorical figures named Fellatio, Cunnilingus, and Bugger.)

But for a number of reasons I think that we've finally come to the point where we have to draw the line, or stand up and be counted, or whatever other phrase is most appropriate for the middle-aged, Sunday-supplement critic I feel myself becoming. It's not a question of law, clearly, nor of hypocrisy or repression (as for hypocrisy, I wish the Free Store Theatre and Grove Press would either stop pretending they're "liberating" us or return to "popular prices," and as for repression, it seems to me that there's as much distorted sexuality in public fellatio as there is on our judicial benches)—it's a question, ultimately, not even of social morality, but of the nature of love, and thus of the ways in which we value ourselves and others.

I'd felt, before seeing *Che,* that my objections would be primarily aesthetic—that the actors, for example, would lunge and grunt, confirming the clichés that seen objectively we're awkward and comic in the sexual act (happily, this turned out to be untrue), or that one would lose all sense of characters, that there'd be an aesthetic lump in the development of the play as we speculated about the actor and actress rather than the hero and heroine (unhappily, this turned out to be true). But at the risk of adding to the solemnity with which everyone in New York is discussing such an essentially frivolous issue, and with a realization that it will take a keener sensibility than mine to distinguish between decadence and innocence (those who've seen Jack Smith's movies will know what I mean), I want to raise a final, ultimate objection to staged sexuality.

Actors and actresses can kiss each other, of course, because although a kiss is a gesture of love, it's also been "socialized" to the extent that it can be performed without personal meaning. Now some people argue that of course kissing on stage was itself once frowned upon, and that in a few years actors and actresses will screw as casually and as impersonally as they now kiss (and if they get pleasure out of it, can their real-life lovers be jealous simply because they enjoy their work?). Obviously, such a futurist society would still regard some fucks as more personal than others, the way we now regard some kisses as more passionate than others. But I wonder, can we treat *everything* as if it were capable of being devoid of personal meaning? Or, to put it another way, don't we need to retain one final refuge, one final last act we will *always* refuse to simulate, one final relationship that can *never* be engaged in for anything but its personal meaning?

Obviously the people in *Che* think not, nor do the people in communes—their argument would be, I presume, why can't indiscriminate sexuality have "personal meaning," why can't we all love and fuck everyone anytime anywhere under any conditions?

Now I'd never attempt to tell anyone how they ought to express their love. But my argument isn't exclusively sexual. When we talk about contemporary invasions of privacy, for instance, I think we touch on only the most obvious and superficial issues when we name the FBI and

IBM. Frankly, I don't so much mind my fingerprints being on file in Washington as I mind those people (we all know them) who in this age of sentimental "candor" feel that they're somehow being dishonest unless they tell you everything about their most intimate life, and who feel you're uptight, if not dishonest, in refusing to respond in kind. It's not a question of manners, or even temperament, but of the ways in which one values some of one's most meaningful experiences—not that we "hide" them, but that we value them properly. If I experience the pain of a friend's betrayal, or the joy of a brief affair, or the agony of watching a beloved person slowly die, these experiences maintain their supreme value—that moment of intimate shared awareness with another person—to the extent that I refuse to dilute or vulgarize them by treating them as casually and openly as I treat more everyday occurrences. I'm not dishonest to A when I don't tell him what happened with B; on the contrary, I'd be dishonest to B by telling A what happened between us—I'd be diluting the intensity of the intimacy by the attempt to share it.

The implications for sexuality are obvious. I'm grateful to Robert Hatch of *The Nation* for having worded it so concisely ("you can photograph only degraded sex, because the photography degrades it") and to Norman Mailer for, among many other things, having made such old-fashioned moralistic positions intellectually respectable. . . .

Ultimately, then, I would argue that actors who perform sexual intercourse on stage are debasing themselves by performing a personally meaningful act for social and artistic goals, by performing an ultimate act for simulated purposes. So I don't so much mind people seeing the sexual act on stage as the sacrifices performers have to make, however willingly, in order for them to see it.

I think it was Freud who said that when two people make love, at least six people are in the room. And of course, sometimes there's only one. But certainly not 120 at ten dollars a head. Two remains the ideal number—for I still believe in halves made whole in the sacrament of sex, halves made whole not in each single romantic act but in a continuing sacred relationship. We are alone in masturbation, alone in orgies—and only in the sexual act with another person, and only when the sexual act has unique meaning because of the beloved identity of that person do we become truly whole. This wholeness is too difficult to achieve, and too valuable when attained, for us casually to risk its reward—which is, after all, finally to become lovers.

## *Cris Hodenfield*

---

# SEX ROCK SYMBOLISM

*You'd better squeeze my lemon babe*
*Until that juice run down my leg*
*(Yeah squeeze it babe*
*you know what I'm talkin bout)*
*I said you'd better squeeze my lemon*
*babe*
*Until that juice runs right down the bed*
*(Yeah, get on with it babe.)*

Robert Johnson
"Terraplane Blues" (1936)

When the Led Zeppelin interject that borrowed lyric, complete with chrome moans, into one of their songs, you can bet the orgasm-hunters in the first fourteen rows sit up and take notice. And the emaciated boys in the three-dollar seats are up and screaming silently too, ostensibly for a heavy guitar player, but really for an amplified, six-string phallus. Rock & roll is sexy business.

At the front of every red-hot band today is the symbol. Mick Jagger sort of got the ball rolling for the white mobs some years back with what the DAR would call dirty lyrics. ("I'm a king bee, baby, lemme come inside your hive.") Before that, it was Elvis (only we had to make up the filthy lyrics for *his* songs), and Jerry Lee Lewis, who qualified as the dirty old man of the rock business when he married his fifteen-year-old cousin. (He really wasn't even divorced from his first wife, either.)

And yes, Chuck Berry, who got some sweet little thing in trouble.

In those cases, we could only rely on reputations of licentiousness for our kicks. Songs with dirty lyrics were banned. ("Baby, Let Me Bang Your Box." And then the immortal "Louie, Louie," with the "I gave her a ten, laid her again" line.)

Today's stars aren't so much concerned with the words as with giving an outright portrayal of the floral-moralled fans' wet dreams. Fans who can't-get-enough-of-it and want-what-he's-got race their throbbing loins off to the ballrooms every weekend for righteous, bold enactment of *lust.*

Lead singers are the first to respond. James Brown ripping his shirt off. Jim Morrison grasping the microphone raunchily, singing lyrics referring to the end of virginity: "I found poetry in your eyes . . . deep and wide . . . break on through to the other side." And then just plain technique: ". . . go real slow, you like it more and more, take it easy baby—take it as it comes."

What with the competition, singers are getting more and more outrageous. Iggy Stooge wraps himself around the microphone stand, projecting the chrome rod from crotch central. In one concert he leapt from the stage and onto a fan. The crowd pushed him back onto the stage. Shortly, he flew back down. "The guy gave me the finger . . . he insulted me. So I either wanted to make it with him, or embarrass him in front of everybody, which I think I did."

Girls can hold up a rock star as the perfect man. He is beautiful, and sexy. And they can look and swoon without having to get down to Doing It. And, in fact, a lot of girls would probably offer their trembling bodies up for sacrifice to the gods. If they could. Give them, however, a boyfriend for their very own, and they'll give up such thoughts of promiscuous yahooing. At a Ten Years After concert I watched one girl turn into protoplasm when singer/guitarist Alvin Lee shouted and groaned the infamous Sonny Boy Williamson lyrics to "Good Morning Little Schoolgirl." She was in a fit as he screamed "I wanna baaaall you . . . I'm GONNA baaaaall you." Musta been half the guys in the house feeling like two cents.

The guitar as a symbol is getting to be old hat. Jimi Hendrix used about every jack-off contortion he could maneuver, and everyone else was immediately fatigued. Still, the guitar is used as a lead instrument in nearly every band, and that is the instrument that carries all the prominent treble. The spotlight is inevitably on its player. Eric Clapton just stands there and plays, but he is a hero in the minds of girls, who think he's sexy, and for guys, who think he plays a mean ax. The admiration of both stems from the same area.

"Lookit," I said, when I saw Jimmy Page of the Led Zeppelin, "he plays with the guitar down around his knees somewhere." Lito, the good old girl who sees such things, pointed out: "No . . . if you look carefully, you'll see that it's held exactly at cock level."

"Oh," I grunted.

But Led Zeppelin is the band that is bringing sex rock to its most outrageous extreme, yet is managing to keep it on a half-humorous level, in the spirit of the good old good-timers like Little Richard.

The female as a rock sex goddess is usually on a different plane. It seems almost impossible to touch her, whereas the male counterparts would seem to be a nervous phone call away for girls. Janis Joplin is presently reigning as the Queen Supreme over the rock scene. Using the all-or-nothing truthing style of Tina Turner, she upsets any healthy guy in her concerts. Just by her dancing and her Texas smile. You think, as she sings in her nerve-grabbing voice, that any girl who sings like that has GOT to love Doing It.

Julie Driscoll dances in an Eastern style, her body coils like a snake, her charm oozes slow Oriental. Grace Slick of the Jefferson Airplane is just plain Sex, yet cooled, distant. Whichever, it's female.

The male sex symbol in rock is taking on a hermaphroditic side. The guitar can be two things at once. The manner in which they are sexy can be both feminine and masculine at the same time. Some cats aren't ashamed at all to say that a performer turns them on. Girls not only admit it, they scream it. The thing is, why doesn't anybody use a megaphone like Rudy Vallee used to? Think of the possibilities.

## *Craig Karpel*

---

# *POP SEX*

Pop art arrayed reality along a parameter of tumescence. Richard Lindner is reality with a hard-on. Claes Oldenberg is reality that has lost its hard-on. Pop sex comes face to glans with the hard-on itself. Cynthia Plastercaster has made twenty-six plaster casts of members of members of rock groups. So let us circumcise our diction: No more phallic symbols, only phalluses. No more Oedipus complexes, only Oedipuses. No more voyeurism: You become what is seen through the keyhole. Make Love, Not War? Does not America possess the resources to make both? As we conquer the world, why not turn the whole of it into an orgone box?

Pop sex is Ted saying to Bob and Carol, "First we'll have an orgy and then we'll go see Tony Bennett": grope therapy.

Pop sex is a split-beaver model in black lace push-'em-up bra, garter belt, seamed nylons and high heels going home from the studio in no bra, pantyhose and clogs.

Pop sex is wearing round Band-Aids over your nipples to keep them from showing through your see-through blouse.

Pop sex is a waitress in a black gauze shirt leaning over to take your beverage order at the Trident restaurant in Sausalito and plopping her boobs in your teriyaki steak and *apologizing*.

Pop sex is a man and a woman in a cigarette ad looking *serious*. "Guess what we were doing just before we lit up these here cigarettes?"

Pop sex is James Simon Kunen having cause to doubt that Lenin was of course as concerned with the relative size of the breasts of female revolutionaries as he.

Pop sex is an article in *Vogue* showing how plastic surgery can cut down on unsightly accumulations of tit and ass, followed by a Marc Eden Bust Development Program ad.

Pop sex is people saying they wouldn't want to shake hands with Philip Roth.

Pop sex is stories about how Vietcong agents among the bar girls of Saigon line their vaginas with razor blades.

Pop sex is Joel Oppenheimer visiting the act of love upon a chicken in "End of the Road." "I'll never," R. Berman wrote the *Village Voice*, "eat another egg." Chicken Delight?

Nick the film-maker had been sitting in front of the Steenberg editing machine for six days, his eyelids propped open with toothpicks, cutting a marriage manual sexploitation flick. (INT. BEDROOM—MS—DAY. A man and a woman are having intercourse. The woman is on top./ Cut to/ INT. DOCTOR'S CONSULTATION RM.—CU—DAY./ DOCTOR: "Particular care must be taken in this position that penetration not be lost.") Now, at three in the morning before he could finally send the film out for the mix he had to make one last cut.

"Lawyer says one thing in here won't pass," said Nick, running the film fast forward. The image on the Steenberg screen was what Masters and Johnson would see if they were, heaven forbid, to drown. "Here," he said, stopping and running it back to where the man gets back on top. The man's doodle was standing at attention. "We've got to cut the hard cock out," Nick sighed. He reached for a razor blade and performed the castration without passion.

He dropped the out-take into a barrel and hung the end from a peg.

"It's a shame, man," said Nick. "Taking out the hard cock fucks up the continuity."

*They are working on it now. It is no larger than a cardiac pacemaker, and runs on rechargeable batteries. The principle is very simple: It bleeps out anything dirty by triggering an electronic pulse generator connected to the auditory nerve. By turning a little knob you can set how funky something has to be before it cuts in. All kids under sixteen will have to wear them unless accompanied by parent or guardian. It will be proscribed for Marine recruits. Inquiries have been received from several enlightened police departments.*

Charles Manson can give a girl an orgasm just by looking at her. That's how all his troubles started.

In San Francisco there is a take-out restaurant called Magnolia Thunderpussy. Magnolia's specialties are the Pineapple Pussy and Barney's Montana Banana. The Pineapple Pussy comprises a pineapple half carved to resemble the venereal mound, filled with ice cream and thatched with grated coconut. Barney's Montana Banana consists of a peeled banana, the near end flanked by two balls of ice cream and sprinkled with coconut.

Freaks in San Francisco are convinced that Magnolia was once busted for serving obscene food.

Jim Morrison of the Doors whipped it out in Miami for thousands of screaming teenyboppers, and thereby confirmed a great and ancient truth: the only way you can get your wang to bulk large in the imagination of thousands of screaming teenyboppers is to keep it in your pants.

In the movie *The Magus* a double was used for Candice Bergen's nude scene. The sex act in movies, in other words, is classified as a stunt.

David Rubinson and Brian Rohan are partners with Bill Graham of the Fillmore ballrooms in the Fillmore Corporation record company. Their office on Market Street in San Francisco is across the street from the Fillmore West, where Graham presents top rock acts. One afternoon a girl walked in and asked Rubinson and Rohan if there were any jobs available at the ballroom. She had long straight dark hair, a pretty face, a shapely body, and nineteen years.

"What do you do?" asked Rohan.

"I don't care. I just want to work at the Fillmore."

"Why do you want to work at the Fillmore?" asked Rubinson.

"Because I want to fuck rock musicians," said the girl.

Rubinson looked at Rohan and Rohan looked at Rubinson and the frame froze.

She is an actress on *Sesame Street,* the educational TV show for little kids. "I'd just as soon wear no bra at all on the air, but I'm supposed to, so I wear just the flimsiest nothing bra I can find, one that my nipples poke through. Why can't kids look at nipples? They suck 'em, don't they?"

We must always have one woman who never reveals herself. We didn't get to see Marilyn Monroe's nipples from the time of the calendar until Bert Stern's portfolio after her death. The current queen of the hidden nipples is Raquel Welch. Her nipples will be her epitaph.

When rats, rabbits and monkeys are dosed with something called p-chlorophenylalanine they commence to go down on each other until totally exhausted. The drug is supposed to counteract a sex-inhibiting chemical in the brain, and it is only a matter of time before humans are going to get into it. (Do any of us doubt that p-chlorophenylalanine will then be accused of causing chromosome damage?)

Scenario: "Abbie Hoffman was indicted today on charges that he and seven other freaks conspired to cross a state line with the intent of adding p-chlorophenylalanine to the water supply and then telling everybody to go fuck themselves."

"I was sitting in the press tent at Woodstock," recalls Paul Krassner, "and this reporter for the New York *Daily News* turns around, cigarette dangling from the corner of his mouth with about an inch of ash, hat pushed back on his head, says out of the corner of his mouth, 'Does anybody know how to spell *bra-less?*' "

Remember *scandals?* Of 200,000,000 Americans, there are only two whom people expect to act with enough circumspection to produce a scandal in the breach: Edward Kennedy and Jacqueline Onassis.

When Alison and I arrived at the hot sulfur baths at Esalen Institute there was no one else around. One side was labeled "MEN'S" and the other "WOMEN'S." We assumed that if we wanted to bathe together we had best go on the men's side—no such thing as a man who objects to bathing naked with a strange woman. Eventually there were eight of us in one tank, five men and three women. We took the waters for an hour and a half. Then we lay on benches and looked at the stars.

Suddenly a face moved into view above us. It belonged to a man carrying a stack of towels. He stood there and looked at Alison and me in our birthday suits, grinning. At length I asked him if there was some way we could be of service.

"I'm afraid I'm going to have to ask you to leave," he said. "There's going to be a seminar using the baths in a few minutes, you see. I'm sure you understand."

I understood. People who are fronting fifty dollars for a seminar in which they sit around naked in baths and get liberated are embarrassed at the sight of people who have paid a buck and a half to simply sit around naked in baths.

I was three thousand miles away before I realized that it never occurred to any of the eight of us that we could all have gone over to the WOMEN'S side. That's liberation for you.

Remember the old Vance Packard riff about cars as surrogate sexual objects? At Chicago's O'Hare airport there is a poster for National Car Rental. The cartoon computer in the ad is saying, "Now it's computerized car dating!"

Coitus as a secret society handshake: "Righteous dope-dealers are like a family," Rikki explains. "The heavies won't do business with someone they don't know until they've dropped acid together, lived under the same roof, eaten out of the same pot, bathed naked, and balled each others' old ladies. Then they know they can trust each other."

*The Filth Mafia, 122 salesmen who are responsible for ninety-seven percent of the dirty jokes made up in the United States each year, meets at the Sheraton Marina Motor Inn in Corpus Christi in a weekend emergency executive session. Sheldon Feinstein, of Applicable Zipper and Fastener, who is probably best remembered for the one about the inventor of Vaseline and the Flying Nun, keynotes the gathering: "The New Morality has pulled the merkin out from under the dirty joke. The other day I was in with a buyer and threw him the one about the cow elephant who missed her period. I crack up and I look over and he's sitting there like a zombie. 'Shelly,' he says to me, 'you've just expressed a very warped viewpoint. How would you and your Pearl like to join us at Axion for a marathon mutual body-exploration sensitivity encounter training seminar? Might straighten you out on some things.'*

*"Which is okay by me, only I ask myself—and I suggest that we all pose this question to ourselves before deciding on our next move—'Can I sell zippers and fasteners while holding hands?'"*

Members of the Weatherman faction of SDS live together in three collectives in Cambridge, Massachusetts. It is said that Weatherwomen are required to ball all the Weathermen in their collective, and vice versa. Neither Weatherman nor Weatherwoman is permitted to ball non-Weatherpeople. "Let me say, at the risk of seeming ridiculous," said Che Guevara, "that a true revolutionary is moved by great feelings of love."

Hugh Hefner's freeze-dried wet dream seems to be holding up, and this is as it should be. To what better use could the libidinal energy of millions of boys mentally un-airbrushing the chicks in *Playboy* be put? The only proven casualties are a piddling number of young bunny fetishists who can't get it up unless they first pluck their girlfriend hairless and brush on a glaze made of orange juice and brown sugar.

A Women's Liberation leader told me that there was no place for men in the Movement. The time had arrived, moreover, for women to stop having sex with men. "How can you justify making it with your oppressor?" she asked.

At the door, her husband pulled me aside. "Maybe there *is* a role for men in the Movement. We should form a sort of Stern Gang to go around assassinating prominent male chauvinists. What do you say?"

I told him I'd have to think about it.

Obscenity is finally being drained out of sex and turning up in politics, where it belongs.

Having nothing to do between moral planes one afternoon I decided to browse through a copy of *The Love Machine*, to look for the good parts. On page sixteen I came to the following: "She could still recall the amazement on his face when he found he had taken a virgin." The saleslady can probably still recall the amazement on my face when I found that Jacqueline Susann sets out to titillate with phrases like "taken a virgin." I brought the book over to the counter and asked the lady to charge it. "Will that be a take or a send?" she asked. "Lady," I said, "believe me when I tell you that it will *not* be a send."

COMING EVENTS:
Vulvar cosmetics, iron out wrinkles.
Computer divorce.
Mammary banks.
Omnisexual movie idols.
Unselfconscious orgasm, like unselfconscious nudity.
Violence peep-shows: "Ovary Action!"
Naked lunches.
Holographic pornography, puts you in the picture.
Parimutuel masturbation.
Unisex public toilets: Go together.

Alison: Men have been following her, making lewd and potentially acrobatic propositions to her, and exposing themselves in front of her as long as she can remember. In a way I have felt flattered by their attentiveness. Here is a woman who could have her pick of perverts, yet she chooses me. What more could a man ask?

The other day she went to Macy's to buy clothes. "Are you married?" asked the salesman at the wrapping desk.

"Yes," she said, assuming that would turn him off.

"Good," he said.

"Pardon?"

"May I ask you a personal question?" he said.

"Shoot."

"Would your husband mind if I went to bed with the two of you?"

"Would my *husband* mind?"

A grey-bunned saleslady stood within earshot, no vital signs on her pan.

Imagine, being loved by a woman so beautiful her most casual suitor would be willing to cornhole me, my abject scrawniness sight unseen, to get a piece of her!

*Charles Winick*

---

# *THE DESEXUALIZED SOCIETY*

The next few generations are likely to be involved in sexual choices and situations that are unprecedented, certainly in American history. These new developments reflect such contradictory factors as the culture's libidinization, depolarization of sex, the flourishing of voyeurism on an unprecedented scale, and the perfection of the technology of genetic engineering. They will pose and are already raising a number of ethical issues of great consequence.

Our social and cultural climate is currently so libidinized that sexual energies, which are probably finite, are being drained to an extraordinary extent by the stimuli in our surroundings. As a result, there could be less and less libido available for traditional kinds of sexual activity involving relationships with people.

Paradoxically, our age of so much libidinization of mass media could be the beginning of an epoch of declining sexual behavior. Why? The few studies that have explored the relationships between sexual attitudes and behavior suggest that a society with liberal attitudes toward sexual expression is likely to have less sexual behavior than a culture that places sanctions on such expression. We may identify as the Godiva Principle the proposition that people will be attracted to sex in proportion to the extent to which it is prohibited. As our society accepts sex more casually, its members may engage in less sexual behavior.

Christiansen and Carpenter in their study, "Value

Discrepancies Regarding Premarital Coitus," compared the relationship between sexual behavior and attitudes in a group of college students among three matched groups in: (a) the intermountain region of the United States; (b) the Midwest; and (c) Denmark. One conclusion of the study was that the Danes had the most liberal attitudes but the least premarital activity. The intermountain students disapproved most explicitly of premarital relations but engaged in such relations more frequently than either of the other groups. We can speculate that the Danes were under the least pressure and therefore engaged in the least sexual behavior.

Additional evidence on the inverse relationship between sexual attitudes and behavior comes from still another survey by Wheeler, who claims that persons of lower socioeconomic status are much more likely than those of the middle or upper classes to express disapproval of nonmarital intercourse. However, male Kinsey interviewees with a grade-school level of education engaged in 10.6 times as much nonmarital intercourse as college men.

It would seem that more liberal sexual attitudes are likely to be correlated with less expression of libido. As we develop such permissive attitudes, we shall probably be less interested in sexual pursuits.

Further clues to the decline in the amount of libido that is available for sexual relationships can be found in studies of the effect of the various forms of the contraceptive pill on the incidence of sexual intercourse. It would be logical to expect the nine million women who currently use the pill would engage in substantially more sexual intercourse than they did before this new contraceptive technique became available. In fact, we find that there is no substantial increase in intercourse on the part of women users of the pill. This nonincrease is occurring even though many women are able to remind themselves each day of their potential as sexual partners and freedom from pregnancy, at the time they ingest the pill. We can speculate that the pill will ultimately lead to a decline in sex relations because like so many other aspects of our culture it routinizes such relations.

Certainly, one of the most extraordinary aspects of American sex roles for the last twenty-five years has been the extent to which masculinity and femininity are becoming blurred and a strange neutering is moving to the center of the stage of at least middle-class life. As sex becomes increasingly depolarized its ability to excite and incite is likely to decline.

Documentation is hardly needed to confirm that men and women increasingly are wearing each other's clothing. Their leisure activities tend not to be sex-linked. In the home, a husband is often a part-time wife, and vice versa. Furniture related to either sex is disappearing, e.g., the leather club chair or the boudoir chair. American men use three times as much fragrance-containing preparations as their wives. Men have been wearing more jewelry at the same time that women are sporting heavy chain belts.

The shoe is the one item of costume that reflects gender most sensitively, perhaps because the foot's position in the shoe is so analogous to the position of the sexual organs during intercourse. As men's shoes have been looking more tapered, higher, and delicate, women's shoes have become stubbier, heavier, and lower.*

The blandness of social-sex roles is reinforced by the neuter quality of much of the environment in our "beige" epoch. Scotches, beers, and blended whiskeys succeed to the extent that they are light or bland. The convenience foods, which have revolutionized our eating habits, are

---

* Charles Winick, "Status, Shoes, and the Life Cycle," *Boot and Shoe Recorder*, 156, October 15, 1959, pp. 100–101.

bland. Even the cigar, once an outpost of strong aroma, has become homogenized.* In a society in which, as Mies van der Rohe said, "less is more," our new buildings tend to be neuter.

This blurring lessens the range of satisfactions available to people and leads to a decline in the quality and quantity of experience available to them. But an even more pressing source of concern for the humanist is the ability of our society to survive at all if the current trend toward depolarization of sex continues. We can state this proposition paradigmatically: (1) A society's ability to sustain itself and to grow creatively is based on the ability of its members to adapt to new situations. (2) Such adaptability is intimately related to the strength of the feelings of personal identity of the people in the society. (3) At the core of any person's sense of identity is his or her awareness of gender. (4) To the extent that a man's sense of masculinity or a woman's feelings of femininity are blurred, such persons will possess a less effective self-concept and be less able to adapt to new situations.

If this paradigm is correct, the depolarization of sex, which is now endemic in this country, could be a prelude to considerable difficulty for us. It could bring about a situation in which the United States may have to choose between our laissez-faire sexual ethic, with its seeming potential for social disaster, and the kind of rigid sex roles that are associated with authoritarianism. It is interesting to note that China and the Soviet Union have adopted a puritan ethic which, if our hypothesis is correct, may actually encourage sexual expression *because* it is so anti-sexual.

The humanist philosophy is clearly opposed to authoritarianism and its attendant rigidity of roles and quashing of individual differences and personal style. Yet,

---

* "The Mellow Cigar," *Barron's*, September 5, 1960, pp. 1–3.

studies of the mental-health implications of various kinds of family structure have tended to conclude that almost any male-female role structure is viable, provided that there is clear division of labor and responsibilities. It is disconcerting to consider the possibility that our open society's ambiguous sex roles may be almost as pathogenic as the rigidities of authoritarianism.

What can the humanist do about this situation? If he agrees that masculinity and femininity should be preserved, he can realize that a number of decisions available to him may contribute to this end. Certainly, we can control the costume and appearance which we present to the world. We can choose the shapes and colors with which we surround ourselves. The toys and dolls which we get for children can reflect gender differences. The names that we give children can communicate maleness or femaleness quite explicitly. We can select leisure activities that make possible an expression of masculinity and femininity. In many other ways, we may exercise options that permit us to avoid being locked into the traditions of the past while still expressing modern forms of masculinity and femininity.

Of the many pop-sociological descriptions of the period since the end of World War II, certainly one of the most apt is the Age of Voyeurism. We see and look and ingest with the eye to a degree that is perhaps unparalleled in human history. If we hypothesize that an increase in one form of sexual expression is related complementarily to other outlets, we can speculate that the great increase in voyeurism is taking place at the expense of coitus and other interpersonal kinds of sex expression.

We know from several studies of readers of peep magazines like *Playboy* and *Confidential* that masturbation is a very popular, and perhaps the most frequent behavioral response to the magazines. It is probable that movies that explicitly present some form of sexual intercourse (e.g., *I Am Curious, Blowup, I A Woman*) will become ever more popular. Such movies and the plethora of printed materials presenting sexual or erotic content may be expected to move people in the direction of masturbating activities rather than interpersonal relations involving sex.

Voyeurism not only is satisfying in itself, as can be inferred from the extraordinary success of *Confidential* and *Playboy,* but it can also inhibit socially constructive action. Thirty-seven New Yorkers heard Kitty Genovese being attacked and murdered and yet did not respond in any way. It is likely that the satisfactions provided by fantasying about Miss Genovese were sufficiently strong to block any impulses toward going or looking outside or phoning the police. Voyeurism is seemingly rewarding enough to inhibit more socially constructive action. There is every reason to expect that our culture will be doing more peeping and less of other kinds of sexual behavior.

Yet another sexual deterrent is the perfection of procedures for freezing sperm and storing it for extended periods. Many routinely successful impregnations with sperm that had been frozen for several years have occurred, and the children show no defects traceable to the manner in which they were conceived.

Procedures are being perfected for removing an unfertilized egg cell from a woman's ovary, fertilizing it in a laboratory flask, and keeping the resulting embryo for an extended period. Such procedures will make it possible for a woman to have a baby by proxy. The egg cell from A could be fertilized in a test tube by sperm from B and nurtured in the body of C, as is taken for granted in breeding sheep and rabbits.

Genetic engineering is an almost inevitable result of the availability of such procedures. What would the humanist position on such matters be? Let us assume that the application of principles of genetic engineering leads to a decision to minimize breeding by a specific ethnic group. How could a humanist deal with such a situation? There would be a clear conflict between the presumed needs of society and unwillingness to label any group as intrinsically and permanently inferior? Yet if we are to abide by principles of genetic engineering, we presumably shall have to make such evaluations. One of the reasons that the United States is the only civilized country without a system of financial allowances for children is the fear of some legislators that the major beneficiaries of such help would be members of some ethnic groups that are believed to be inferior. Once the genetic counselor begins to advise potential mates and combines his skills with computer capabilities, romantic love as we know it is doomed. Life will not only be different, but it will be considerably delibidinized.

The several trends noted above would seem to be working toward an overall decline in sex expression. A key ethical issue, then, in the next several decades would seem to be why people should engage in the various kinds of sexual behavior that involves others. The strength of the sexual drive is not self-sustaining, and as the culture drains more and more libido, people will have less occasion for engaging in sexual relations. It certainly will not be necessary for purposes of procreation. Presumably other levels of personal satisfaction will become important.

The affirmation and expression represented by sexual relations with others are human values that are too fulfilling to abandon. A humanist view of the sexual scene could encourage its adherents to make every effort to counter the trends that threaten to make sexual expression, in terms of relations with others, an historical subject. The very ability of our society to survive is at stake.

## *Dan Greenburg*

---

# *"WAS IT GOOD FOR YOU, TOO?"*

"Good afternoon," said the interviewer pleasantly to the blond young man on the other side of the desk.

"Good afternoon," said Perlmutter.

There was an uncomfortable pause, which the interviewer savored, studying Perlmutter's discomfort.

"I'm here about the experiment," said Perlmutter, "the one you mentioned in the ad."

"Ah yes, the ad," said the interviewer.

"I . . . uh, trust that I'm in the right place?"

"Oh, you're in the right place," said the interviewer, smiling blandly. "You want to be in one of our sex experiments, isn't that right?"

"Well, I . . . yes," said Perlmutter.

"You're a student here?"

"Yes. Pre-med."

"Ah."

"I, uh, trust that there are still . . . openings? In the program, I mean?"

"Tell me," said the interviewer, doodling a possibly erotic doodle on a pad in front of him, "why are you volunteering to participate in a sex experiment?"

"What's the difference?" said Perlmutter.

"I assure you," said the interviewer patronizingly, "we have no wish to pry into your personal affairs, except as they may relate to our business here at the project. Due to the, ah, unusual nature of these particular experiments, we like to have as much information as possible on the people we use, as an aid in determining the potential success or failure of our work."

"I see."

"Now then, what made you volunteer?"

"Well," said Perlmutter, reddening, "outside of the obvious professional interest I have in such activity . . ."

"Yes," said the interviewer, "outside of that."

"Well, quite frankly, I consider myself somewhat of a . . . actually, *quite* a good . . . uh, well, at least a fairly adequate lover, and . . ."

"And . . . ?"

"And also, I thought it might be a good way of meeting girls," he blurted out in some confusion.

"You understand, of course," said the interviewer, "that you will never be permitted to learn the identity of the young lady or ladies whom you will, ah, meet during the course of the experiment?"

"I understand," said Perlmutter.

The buxom middle-aged woman in the white lab coat looked up from her papers and motioned Perlmutter into a chair. The hair on her head was dark, frizzy, and pubic. He wondered if the hair in her bush was straight, silky, and blond. She pointed to the forms he held in his lap. He handed them over.

"Perlmutter?" said Dr. Bronson, adjusting her glasses and glancing quickly and professionally over the forms.

"Right."

"Says here you're volunteering for a straight Hetero-Norm-Coital set-up. That right?"

"Uh, right."

"No interest in any . . . in anything more exotic?"

"What do you mean?"

"What I mean to say is that we are concerned in this experiment with the full range of human sexual activity, not just a small segment of it. As I'm sure you realize, not everybody in the world gets his kicks from just coital contact, nor from contact with a partner of a sex opposite to his own, nor from just one partner at a time, nor even from exclusively *human* partners."

"Well, naturally," said Perlmutter.

"So what I am asking is whether, as you've indicated on this form here, you truly wish to restrict your participation in this experiment to a straight coital encounter with just one human partner at a time of the opposite sex?"

"Oh. Well, yes," said Perlmutter, "I believe so."

"All right," said Dr. Bronson.

"At least for the first one," Perlmutter added, not wishing to be thought a total square.

Dr. Bronson pursed her lips and thoughtfully injected a pencil into her mouth. "You realize, of course," she said at length, "that there are going to be a number of factors present in this experiment of a somewhat distracting nature."

"I realize that," said Perlmutter.

"You realize that you are going to be observed at all times during the experiment by a team of scientists and a battery of delicate and comprehensive measuring equipment."

"I realize that," said Perlmutter.

"Do you think you will be distracted by being observed while in the act of coitus? That is, do you think it will, ah, impair your function?"

"I doubt it," said Perlmutter. "I have been observed before."

"Oh?"

"I mean, I did live in a fraternity house for almost four years."

At eight-thirty on a brisk Saturday evening in fall, Perlmutter arrived at the Extension Offices of the Project on Psychophysiological Research for his twelfth and, he hoped, final briefing.

After sitting for about ten minutes on a folding chair in an otherwise deserted and sparsely-furnished waiting room, the translucent glass door marked STAFF ONLY opened, and a young nurse in a white uniform gave him a pleasant but perfunctory smile.

"We're ready for you now, Mr. Perlmutter," she said.

Perlmutter walked through the door into an examination room with an elevated table, upholstered in brown leather.

"Are you Clothed Foreplay, Semi-Clothed, or Nude?" said the nurse.

"Pardon?"

The nurse consulted her metal clipboard.

"Perlmutter," she said. "Ah yes. You're Semi-Clothed. Would you kindly remove your jacket, tie, shirt, shoes, and trousers, and then follow me into the next room?"

"I've already *had* my physical examination," said Perlmutter, fearing some clerical error. "What examination is this?"

"Oh, this is no examination," said the nurse, "this is the biggie."

"The what?"

"The biggie. This is *it*. Tonight's the night," she said with a wink.

"Tonight?" said Perlmutter. "I had no idea it was tonight. Nobody told me."

"That's the way they're handling them now," said the nurse. "Hurry now, and give me your clothes. They're waiting for you, and they're already four minutes behind schedule."

Perlmutter stepped through the door in his undershorts and was only partially surprised to meet two middle-aged men and one woman, all wearing glasses and white coats, and holding aluminum clipboards.

The woman he recognized as Dr. Bronson. The older of the two men was Dr. Jaspers, the co-conductor of the experiments. The other man was evidently some sort of technician.

At the far end of the room stood a bank of complicated machines, covered with dials and wires. In the middle of the room was a large bed with the covers turned down, as if by a hotel chambermaid. A little night table with a crocheted doily and a pitcher of some cold drink or other was apparently somebody's attempt to balance the clinical atmosphere with a touch of domesticity.

"Perlmutter?" said Dr. Jaspers.

"Yes."

"Good. Nurse, send in Miss Ras—Send in our other participant."

A pleasant-looking slender girl of about twenty entered the room with what Perlmutter judged to be a surprising amount of aplomb, under the circumstances. She had long straight hair of a nondescript brown color, and wore bikini panties, a black brassiere, and glasses.

"I took the liberty of having her remove the stockings and garter belt to save time, doctor," said the nurse, and then turned anxiously to Perlmutter. "Unless that excites you?" she said.

"Oh. Stockings? No, that's O.K.," said Perlmutter.

"Very well now," said Dr. Jaspers, "will you both please step over to the bed?"

Perlmutter and the young woman approached the bed and looked at each other shyly.

"I guess we're supposed to sit down on it or something," said Perlmutter.

They sat down on the bed and had some difficulty deciding how close to sit to each other. For want of something else to do, Perlmutter puffed up one of the pillows.

Dr. Bronson approached the bed with several coils of wire, a roll of tape, and a small bottle of clear liquid.

"Don't pay any attention to me, kids," she said. "Just get started."

"What are these things?" said Perlmutter as Dr. Bronson began fitting an electrode to the left corner of his mouth.

"Various technical devices to measure your physiological responses. Don't pay any attention to them. Just get the ball rolling."

"Look, these things are going to get in the way," said Perlmutter out of the right corner of his mouth, as Dr. Bronson began to attach a second electrode to his armpit.

"They shouldn't," said Dr. Bronson, taping a third electrode to his chest.

"I'm not sure I like these things at all," said Perlmutter.

"Then why don't *you* start things off, dear?" said Dr. Bronson to the young woman.

Obligingly, the girl reached out, placed her arms around Perlmutter's neck and drew him down on top of her. Miraculously, and in spite of any anxieties to the contrary, Perlmutter felt himself beginning to get aroused.

"Hello there," he said to the girl, feeling somehow they should have been introduced, at least with pseudonyms.

"Hi," said the young lady, and bit his earlobe.

"Would you please remove the bra," said Dr. Bronson, "I need a nipple here."

"O.K.," said Perlmutter sheepishly, and with a modicum of difficulty unhooked the young lady's brassiere.

She had rather nice ones, he thought, and did a little test of his own.

"If it's all the same to you," said Dr. Bronson, "I'd prefer that you worked on the right one. The left one is mine."

"Oh. Sorry." Perlmutter quickly moved to his proper station.

"Mmmm," said the girl.

"Feel nice?" said Perlmutter.

"I get an excitation reading of three-point-two," said the lab man, scrutinizing his dials. "I call that feeling pretty nice."

"Let's push on now," said Dr. Bronson. "I need the crotch."

Perlmutter, slightly irritated at the older woman's back-seat driving, slid his hands over the young lady's hips and pulled down her panties. Once more, he felt a surge of excitement. He began to run his tongue lightly across her collarbone and down her rib cage to the waist.

"Excuse me," said Dr. Bronson from somewhere below. "You kids may have all night, but we're on a schedule here." She unceremoniously eased Perlmutter out of his shorts.

Perlmutter and the young woman looked politely beyond each other's nakedness as Dr. Bronson continued to attach electrodes.

"Do you, uh, come here often?" said Perlmutter, and realized immediately the inanity of his question.

"I've been here about twelve times," said the girl.

"Oh. Me too. How did you happen to vol—Hey!" he said suddenly to Dr. Bronson, "What the hell are you gluing to me *there?*"

"Merely an intrauterine camera," said Dr. Bronson. "Don't get so upset."

"Listen," said Perlmutter, "how do you expect me to—"

"Did you or did you not tell me in examination that you have extraordinary powers of concentration?"

"Well, sure, but there's a limit to—"

He felt a gentle, reassuring hand on his shoulder.

"It's all right, don't worry about it," said the young lady. She had a marvelous smile. "We'll do it anyway. I'll help you."

Perlmutter looked at her gratefully. Then she closed her eyes and he kissed her for the first time. She was really an exceptional kisser. Perlmutter wondered if he were going to fall in love.

"You know," he said, "you're really very nice." He began to move his hands over the soft, warm curves of her body.

"So are you," she said.

"You have lovely skin," he said.

"You have a very . . . wiry chest," she said.

"You have static on your oral-audio circuits," said the lab man.

"Listen," said Perlmutter, "you know you really do look awfully familiar to me. Are you sure we haven't met before?"

"I doubt it, I never forget a face," said the girl.

"The talking is what's giving you your static," said Dr. Jaspers. "Cut out the cross-talk, would you?"

"According to the secretiometer, she does not look very excited to me," said Dr. Bronson. "Young man, do you think you could pep up your pace a little?"

With more than a little annoyance, Perlmutter pepped up his pace.

Quietly, steadily, doggedly, he worked over the young woman's body until, perhaps ten minutes later, she began to moan with pleasure. And for a moment he forgot all about the electrodes, the wires, the machines, the doctors, and the intrauterine camera.

"Contact," said somebody on the other side of the room, but neither he nor the girl paid any attention. With deliberate, rhythmic, somewhat masterful motions, Perlmutter was bringing her higher and higher, closer and closer to the summit.

"Do you like it this way?" he whispered.

"Oh, yes. I never knew it could be like this," she said.

"You really think I'm that good?"

"Marvelous. The best."

"Honest? You really mean it?"

"Marvelous," she groaned. "One of the two best sexual experiences I've had in my entire life. Ouch! What are you doing?"

"Who was the other?"

"What?"

"You said I was one of the *two* best. Who was the other?"

"Ow! Hey! What do you mean? What does it matter?"

"I have to know."

"A guy in Wisconsin. I don't even remember his—Hey, now cut that out—I'm not kidding!"

"Cut that out," said Dr. Bronson. "You volunteered for Normal-Coital, not Sado-Maso, remember? You're going beyond the parameters of this experiment."

"What did the guy in Wisconsin do that was so great?" said Perlmutter.

"I don't remember. It was a long time ago."

"Did he do *this?*"

"Hey!" said the young lady, "you're giving me marks."

"Hey!" said the technician, "you're giving me negative feedback on my white reference!"

"Did he?" said Perlmutter.

"Ooh!" said the young lady. "No, I don't think he did *that.*"

"We are not equipped to measure what you are doing now, young man," said Dr. Bronson, "although it is very interesting. Perhaps you would wish to change your category and start over again with another partner?"

"I've got a beauty for him in the morning group," said Dr. Jaspers. "She wears leather underwear."

"This one is just fine," said Perlmutter.

"Oooh," said the young lady again.

"Am I still one of the two?" said Perlmutter.

"Ooooohhhhhhhh. My God. No."

"Then tell me."

"Oooohhhhhh."

"Tell me."

"Ohhh, you are—you're the best. My God."

"Unless you cut that out right now and go back to the regular experiment, the whole thing is off," said Dr. Jaspers.

"The best, eh?" said Perlmutter.

"God, yes."

"Good," said Perlmutter, "that's better. That's much better."

"I'm not kidding you, young man, I'm going to stop this experiment," said Dr. Jaspers. "That means you both forfeit full monetary compensation, you know."

"Am I going to see you again?" said Perlmutter.

"That's not allowed!" said Dr. Bronson.

"Yes! Yes!" said the young lady.

"Often?" said Perlmutter.

"I forbid this! I forbid it!" yelled Dr. Jaspers. "Dr. Bronson, remove the electrodes—this experiment is canceled!"

"As often as you want," said the young lady, "Oh God God God God God."

"And will you stop seeing anybody else you're now seeing?" said Perlmutter.

Somebody was pulling wires off Perlmutter's body, but he hardly noticed.

"Will you?" said Perlmutter.

"I'm sorry to bother you," said Dr. Bronson, "but I need that camera back now."

"*Will* you?" said Perlmutter.

"Yes, yes, my God—yes!" said the young lady.

"The camera, please. We have another couple waiting."

Dr. Bronson pulled them forcibly apart, yanked Perlmutter off the bed and half dragged him toward the examination room where he had first gotten undressed. The young lady was still sobbing in the background as Dr. Bronson, puffing hard from exertion, pushed Perlmutter into the examination room and slammed the door behind them.

"Well," Dr. Bronson gasped, "that was some demonstration. Some cute little act you've got there. A few more hot-pantsed lunkheads like you, and the entire project goes out of the window."

"I'm sorry," said Perlmutter, "I just got carried away. That happens to me sometimes."

After he got dressed Perlmutter waited around outside the building for ten or fifteen minutes, but the girl never appeared. Perlmutter figured she'd probably left by another entrance and so he went on home.

Leafing through a telephone book in his rooming house, he looked for her in vain. All he really knew about her was the first syllable of her last name which Dr. Jaspers had let slip when she'd first entered the room: RAS—. He opened the book to RAS—once more but once more he didn't know where to begin calling. It could have been anything: Rasmussen, Raspberry, Rasputin, Raskolnikov, anything.

Besides, what could he say to the people he called—"Hello, would you be kind enough to tell me whether you are the person I made love to earlier this evening at the University?"

No, it wasn't worth the embarrassment. He'd just have to forget about her, that's all. It was probably just as well. She was probably emotionally unacceptable as a serious romantic partner anyway. She was probably so hung up she couldn't make it without at least three people looking on. He could just see himself making frantic phone calls to round up a trio of voyeurs every time he wanted to make love to her. No, he was better off without her. In fact, he was relieved to be rid of her. After all, *who needed the kind of a nut you would have to be to volunteer for a sex experiment anyway?*

## *Susan Lydon*

---

# *LIBERATING WOMAN'S ORGASM*

Tiresias, who had been both man and woman, was asked, as Ovid's legend goes, to mediate in a dispute between Jove and Juno as to which sex got more pleasure from lovemaking. Tiresias unhesitatingly answered that women did. Yet in the intervening 2000 years between Ovid's time and our own, a mythology has been built up which not only holds the opposite to be true, but has made this belief an unswerving ideology dictating the quality of relations between the sexes. Women's sexuality, defined by men to benefit men, has been downgraded and perverted, repressed and channeled, denied and abused until women themselves, thoroughly convinced of their sexual inferiority to men, would probably be dumbfounded to learn that there is scientific proof that Tiresias was indeed right.

The myth was codified by Freud as much as anyone else. In *Three Essays on the Theory of Sexuality,* Freud formulated his basic ideas concerning feminine sexuality: for little girls, the leading erogenous zone in their bodies is the clitoris; in order for the transition to womanhood to be successful, the clitoris must abandon its sexual primacy to the vagina; women in whom this transition has not been complete remain clitorally oriented, or "sexually anaesthetic," and "psychosexually immature." In the context of Freud's total psychoanalytic view of women—that they are not whole human beings but mutilated males who long all their lives for a penis and must struggle to reconcile themselves to its lack—the requirement of a transfer of erotic sensation from clitoris to vagina became a prima facie case for their inevitable sexual inferiority. In Freud's logic, those who struggle to become what they are not must be inferior to that to which they aspire.

Freud himself admitted near the end of his life that his knowledge of women was inadequate. "If you want to know more about femininity, you must interrogate your own experience, or turn to the poets, or wait until science can give you more profound and more coherent information," he said; he also hoped the female psychoanalysts who followed him would be able to find out more. But the post-Freudians adhered rigidly to the doctrine of the master, and, as with most of his work, what Freud hoped would be taken as a thesis for future study became instead a kind of canon law.

While the neo-Freudians haggled over the correct reading of the Freudian bible, watered-down Freudianism was wending its way into the cultural mythology via Broadway plays, novels, popular magazines, social scientists, marriage counselors and experts of various kinds who found it useful in projecting desired images of woman. The superiority of the vaginal over the clitoral orgasm was particularly useful as a theory, since it provided a convenient basis for categorization: clitoral women were deemed immature, neurotic, bitchy and masculine; women who had vaginal orgasms were maternal, feminine, mature and normal. Though frigidity should technically be defined as total inability to achieve orgasm, the orthodox Freudians (and pseudo-Freudians) preferred to define it as inability to achieve vaginal orgasm, by which definition, in 1944, Edmond Bergler adjudged between seventy and eighty percent of all women frigid. The clitoral vs. vaginal debate raged hot and heavy among the sexologists—Kinsey's writings stressed the importance of the clitoris to female orgasm and contradicted Bergler's statistics—but it became clear that there was something indispensable to society in the Freudian view which allowed it to remain unchallenged in the public consciousness.

In 1966, Dr. William H. Masters and Mrs. Virginia E. Johnson published *Human Sexual Response,* a massive clinical study of the physiology of sex. Briefly and simply, the Masters and Johnson conclusions about the female orgasm, based on observation of and interviews with 487 women, were these:

1) That the dichotomy of vaginal and clitoral orgasms is entirely false. Anatomically, all orgasms are centered in the clitoris, whether they result from direct manual pressure applied to the clitoris, indirect pressure resulting from the thrusting of penis during intercourse, or generalized sexual stimulation of other erogenous zones like the breasts.

2) That women are naturally multi-orgasmic; that is, if a woman is immediately stimulated following orgasm, she is likely to experience several orgasms in rapid succession. This is not an exceptional occurrence, but one of which most women are capable.

3) That while women's orgasms do not vary in kind, they vary in intensity. The most intense orgasms experienced by the research subjects were by masturbatory manual stimulation, followed in intensity by manual stimulation by the partner; the least intense orgasms were experienced during intercourse.

4) That there is an "infinite variety in female sexual response" as regards intensity and duration of orgasms.

To anyone acquainted with the body of existing knowledge of feminine sexuality, the Masters and Johnson findings were truly revolutionary and liberating in the extent to which they demolished the established myths. Yet two years after the study was published, it seems hardly to have made any impact at all. Certainly it is not for lack of information that the myths persist; *Human Sexual Response*, despite its weighty scientific language, was an immediate best seller, and popular paperbacks explicated it to millions of people in simpler language and at a cheaper price. The myths remain because a male-dominated American culture has a vested interest in their continuance.

Before Masters and Johnson, men defined feminine sexuality in a way as favorable to themselves as possible. If woman's pleasure was obtained through the vagina, then she was totally dependent on the man's erect penis to achieve orgasm; she would receive her satisfaction only as a concomitant of man's seeking his. With the clitoral orgasm, woman's sexual pleasure was independent of the male's, and she could seek her satisfaction as aggressively as the man sought his, a prospect which didn't appeal to too many men. The definition of feminine sexuality as normally vaginal, in other words, was a part of keeping women down, of making them sexually as well as economically, socially and politically subservient.

In retrospect, particularly with the additional perspective of our own times, Freud's theory of feminine sexuality appears to be an historical rationalization for the realities of Victorian society. A prisoner of the Victorian ethos, Freud had to play the paterfamilias. Freud's analysis implied that woman's low status had not been conferred upon her by men, but by God, who created her without a penis.

The superiority of the vaginal orgasm seems almost a demoniac determination on Freud's part to complete the Victorians' repression of feminine eroticism, to stigmatize the remaining vestiges of pleasure felt by women and thus make them unacceptable to the women themselves. For there were still women whose sexuality hadn't been completely destroyed, as evidenced by one Dr. Isaac Brown Baker, a surgeon who performed numerous clitoridectomies on women to prevent the sexual excitement which, he was convinced, caused "insanities," "catalepsy," "hysteria," "epilepsy" and other diseases. The Victorians needed to repress sexuality for the success of Western industrialized society; in particular, the total repression of woman's sexuality was crucial to ensure her subjugation. So the Victorians honored only that aspect of sexuality which was necessary to the survival of the species—the male ejaculation; made women submissive to sex by creating a mystique of the sanctity of motherhood; and, supported by Freud, passed on to us the heritage of the double standard.

When Kinsey laid to rest the part of the double standard that maintained women got no pleasure at all from sex, everyone cried out that there was a sexual revolution afoot. But such talk, as usual, was deceptive. Morality, outside the marriage bed, remained the same, and children were socialized as though Kinsey had never described what they would be like when they grew up. Boys were taught that they should get their sex where they could find it, "go as far" as they could. On the old assumption that women were asexual creatures, girls were taught that since they needed sex less than boys did, it was up to them to impose sexual restraints. In whatever sex education adolescents did manage to receive, they were told that men had penises and women vaginas; the existence of the clitoris was not mentioned, and *pleasure* in sex was never discussed at all.

Adolescent boys growing up begging for sexual crumbs from girls frightened for their "reputations"—a situation that remains unchanged to this day—hardly constitutes the vanguard of a sexual revolution. However, the marriage manual craze that followed Kinsey assumed that a lifetime of psychological destruction could, with the aid of a little booklet, be abandoned after marriage, and that husband and wife should be able to make sure that the wife was not robbed of her sexual birthright to orgasm, just so long as it was *vaginal* (though the marriage manuals did rather reluctantly admit that since the clitoris was the most sexually sensitive organ in the female body, a little clitoral stimulation was in order), and so long as their orgasms were *simultaneous.*

The effect of the marriage manuals of course ran counter to their ostensible purpose. Under the guise of frankness and sexual liberation, they dictated prudery and restraint. Sex was made so mechanized, detached and intellectual that it was robbed of its sensuality. Man became a spectator of his own sexual experience. And the marriage manuals put new pressure on women. The swing was from repression to preoccupation with the orgasm. Men took the marriage manuals to mean that their sexuality would be enhanced by bringing women to orgasm and, again coopting feminine sexuality for their own ends, they put pressure on women to perform. The marriage manuals' endorsement of the desirability of vaginal orgasm insured that women would be asked not only, "Did you come?" but also, "Did you conform to Freud's conception of a psychosexually mature woman, and thereby validate my masculinity?"

Appearances notwithstanding, the age-old taboos against conversation about personal sexual experience haven't yet been broken down. This reticence has allowed the mind-manipulators of the media to create myths of sexual supermen and superwomen. So the bed becomes a competitive arena, where men and women measure themselves against these mythical rivals, while simultaneously trying to live up to the ecstasies promised them by the marriage manuals and the fantasies of the media ("If the earth doesn't move for me, I must be missing something"). Our society has made sex a sport, with its record-breakers, its judges, its rules and its spectators.

As anthropologists have shown, woman's sexual response is culturally conditioned; historically, women defer to whatever model of their sexuality is offered them by men. So the sad thing for women is that they have participated in the destruction of their own eroticism. Women have helped make the vaginal orgasm into a status symbol in a male-dictated system of values. A woman would now perceive her preference for clitoral orgasm as a "secret shame," ignominious in the eyes of other women as well as those of men. This internalization can be seen in literature: Mary McCarthy and Doris Lessing's writings on orgasm do not differ substantially from Ernest Hemingway's, and Simone de Beauvoir, in *The Second Sex*, refers to vaginal orgasm as the only "normal satisfaction."

One factor that has made this possible is that female sexuality is subtle and delicate, conditioned as much by the emotions as by physiology and sociology. Masters and Johnson proved that the orgasm experienced during intercourse, the misnamed vaginal orgasm, did not differ *anatomically* from the clitoral orgasm. But this should not be seen as their most significant contribution to the sexual emancipation of women. A difference remains in the *subjective* experience of orgasm during intercourse and orgasm apart from intercourse. In the complex of emotional factors affecting feminine sexuality, there is a whole panoply of pleasures: the pleasure of being penetrated and filled by a man, the pleasure of sexual communication, the pleasure of affording a man his orgasm, the erotic pleasure that exists even when sex is not terminated by orgasmic release. Masters and Johnson's real contribution was to show this "infinite variety in female sexual response"; that one experience is not better than another, but merely different.

There is no doubt that Masters and Johnson were fully aware of the implications of their study to the sexual liberation of women. As they wrote, "With orgasmic physiology established, the human female now has an undeniable opportunity to develop realistically her own sexual response levels." Two years later this statement seems naive and entirely too optimistic. Certainly the sexual problems of our society will never be solved until there is real and unfeigned equality between men and women. This idea is usually misconstrued: sexual liberation for women is wrongly understood to mean that women will adopt all the forms of masculine sexuality. As in the whole issue of women's liberation, that's really not the point. Women don't aspire to imitate the mistakes of men in sexual matters, to view sexual experiences as conquest and ego-enhancement, to use other people to serve their own ends. But if the Masters and Johnson material is allowed to filter into the public consciousness, hopefully to replace the enshrined Freudian myths, then woman at long last will be allowed to take the first step toward her emancipation: to define and enjoy the forms of her own sexuality.

*Leslie Farber*

---

## *THE TRADITIONAL O*

The political clamor for equal rights for woman at the turn of the century could not fail to join with sexology to endow her with an orgasm, equal in every sense to the male orgasm. It was agreed that she was entitled to it just as she was entitled to the vote. Moreover, if she were deprived of such release her perturbation would be as unsettling to her nervous system as similar frustration was thought to be for the man. Equal rights were to be erotically consummated in simultaneous orgasm. On the one hand it was unhealthy for her to be deprived of release and, on the other hand, psychoanalysis decreed that an important sign of her maturity as woman was her ability to achieve it. In other words, without orgasm she was neurotic to begin with or neurotic to end with.

Though simultaneous orgasm seemed to be a necessary consequence of equal rights, the problem remained that in matters of lust more than a decree or amendment was required for such an achievement. True, the sexologists were most generous with instruction, but each citizen has had to discover over and over again the degree to which he is caught in the futile struggle to will what could not be willed — at the same time that he senses the real absurdity of the whole willful enterprise. The lover learns, as his indoctrination progresses, to observe uneasily and even resist his rush of pleasure if it seems he is to be premature. When no amount of resolution can force his pleasure to recede, he learns to suffer his release and then quickly prod himself to an activity his body's exhaustion opposes. In other words, he learns to take his moment in stride, so to speak, omitting the deference these moments usually call forth and then without breaking stride get to his self-appointed and often fatiguing task of tinkering with his mate—always hopeful that his ministrations will have the appearance of affection. While she is not likely to be deceived by such dutiful exercises, she nevertheless wishes for both their sakes that her body at least will be deluded into fulfilling its franchise.

As far as I know, little attention was paid to the female orgasm before the era of sexology. Where did the sexologists find it? Did they discover it or invent it? Or both? I realize it may seem absurd to raise such questions about events as unmistakable as those witnessed in our laboratory. But I cannot believe that previous centuries were not up to our modern delights; nor can I believe it was the censorship imposed by religion which suppressed the supreme importance of the female orgasm. My guess, which is not subject to laboratory proof, is that the female orgasm was always an occasional, though not essential, part of a woman's whole sexual experience. I also suspect that it appeared with regularity or predictability only during masturbation when the more human qualities of her life with her mate were absent. Further, her perturbation was unremarkable and certainly bearable when orgasm did not arrive, for our lovers had not yet been enlightened as to the disturbances resulting from the obstruction or distortion of sexual energies. At this stage her orgasm had not yet been abstracted and isolated from the totality of her pleasures, and enshrined as the meaning and measure of her erotic life. She was content with the mystery and variety of her difference from man, and in fact would not have had it otherwise. Much that I have said, if we leave aside the erotomanias which have always been with us, applies to the male of previous centuries. For him, too, the moment of orgasm was not abstracted in its objective form from the whole of his erotic life and then idealized. And he too preferred the mystery of difference, the impact of human contingency, becoming obsessed with the sheer anatomy and mechanics of orgasm only when all else was missing, as in masturbation.

Theological parallelism is a treacherous hobby, especially when we deal with movements flagrantly secular. Nevertheless, the manner in which lovers now pursue their careers as copulating mammals—adopting whatever new refinements sexology devises, covering their faces yet exposing their genitals—may remind us of older heresies which, through chastity or libertinism, have pressed toward similar goals; one heretical cult went so far as to worship the serpent in the Garden of Eden. But the difference between these older heresies and modern science—and there is a large one—must be attributed to the nature of science itself, which—if we accept such evidence as the Lambeth Conference—by means of its claims to objectivity can invade religion and ultimately all of life to a degree denied the older heresies. So, with the abstraction, objectification, and idealization of the female orgasm we have come to the last and perhaps most important clause of the contract which binds our lovers to their laboratory home, there to will the perfection on earth which cannot be willed, there to suffer the pathos which follows all such strivings toward heaven on earth.

*Derek Wright*

---

# SEX:
# INSTINCT OR APPETITE?

Sex is usually thought of as one of the instincts, and as such classed with hunger and thirst. It is notoriously difficult to define precisely what an instinct is; but in everyday usage it refers to an urge which directs behavior and which is generated by a biological need. On the analogy with hunger and thirst, it follows that deprivation of sexual satisfaction should lead to an increase in need. So when someone apparently does not go in for sexual activity, we are left wondering what he does about this need. Healthy living, we presume, requires regular sexual "outlet." When this is not possible we expect the sex urge to find more indirect and devious ways of expressing itself.

Until recently psychologists themselves held a view similar to this. Behaviorist psychologists classed sex as a primary drive and they assumed that the principles which govern behavior instigated by hunger will also apply to sexual behavior. Freud's view of sex is similar. He defines "libido" as "psychic energy"—the tension or excitation that is seeking discharge through behavior. At any particular time, according to Freud, libido exists in a finite quantity and it originates in internal bodily processes. It differs from other instinctual energies, he says, in that it is highly displaceable, and easily repressed, sublimated or diverted into forms of behavior which have no obvious connection with sexuality. This highly mobile quality of the libido enabled Freud to discover its presence in creative art, science and so on.

In the last decade or so, there has been a burgeoning of research in this field, much of it directed toward the biology and physiology of sex. Discrepancies have emerged between the way sex seems to act, and the way hunger or thirst do.

Admittedly, the determining influence of genetic structure has been demonstrated in the sexual behavior of several animal species. Thus, in mice, genetics seem to account for differences in the number of times the penis is inserted before ejaculation is reached, and in the amount of time before the sex drive is recovered after ejaculation. Again in monkeys, erection of the penis and ejaculation can be produced by electrical stimulation of the brain.

Such research shows how important the built-in biological factors are. But their influence is neither simple nor direct, particularly in human beings. Sexual arousal depends much more on external stimuli than hunger or thirst does. Even the hormones that are secreted by the glands seem only to make sexual arousal possible when appropriate stimulation occurs, rather than to induce it directly themselves. There is evidence, too, that once a pattern of sexual behavior is well established in an animal, it tends to become "autonomous"—i.e., it becomes a little bit less dependent on its biological basis. Rats castrated as adults will nonetheless copulate when the relevant stimuli, such as a female in heat, are there.

Most important is the evidence of evolutionary development in sexual behavior. The higher up we go in the phylogenetic scale, the more the cortex (the upper brain) is involved. In lower species, what external stimuli will release sexual activity is largely determined by the innate genetic structure of the animal; in man, however, they are heavily conditioned by culture and circumstances. The Harlows showed that monkeys which were grossly deprived of social contact virtually lacked sexual activity when they became adult. Psychiatric observation suggests that human sexual behavior is subtly shaped by the nature of the social attachments formed during a person's development.

In man, as in lower species, secretions of hormones bring the body to functional readiness at puberty; but the relation between hormonal balance and sex drive is obscure. Some studies have found that women who are undergoing androgen therapy report enhanced sexual interest, but the evidence is meager; and for men it is quite inconclusive.

Wide individual differences are observable in sexual interest. Whether a person has sexual intercourse often or less often, he can adapt fairly readily to either situation without his general efficiency being affected. In Michael Schofield's survey of the sexual behavior of adolescents, less than half the boys reported enjoying their first experience of sexual intercourse (despite the fact that apparently the great majority reached orgasm) and less than a third of the girls. It did not appear to be a particularly thrilling event for either sex.

Thus, it is misleading to see sex in human beings as a simple response to a biological need. It is much closer to the truth to think of it as an acquired appetite or taste. Professor F. A. Beach, one of the most distinguished of researchers into sexual behavior, makes the point forcibly:

> No genuine tissue or biological needs are generated by sexual abstinence. It used to be believed that prolonged sexual inactivity in adulthood resulted in the progressive accumulation of secretions within the accessory sex glands, and that nerve impulses from these distended receptacles gave rise to sexual urges. Modern evidence negates this hypothesis. . . . What is commonly confused with a primary drive associated with sexual need is in actuality sexual appetite, and this has little or no relation to biological or physio-

> logical needs. . . . Sexual appetite is . . . a product of experience, actual or vicarious. The adolescent boy's periodic preoccupation with sexual matters is traceable to psychological stimuli, external and phantasied, and is not dependent upon his recently matured reproductive glands. His erotic urges stem more from socio-cultural factors than from those of the strictly physiological nature.

This approach to sexual motivation has been taken up and elaborated at length by others (by K. R. Hardy and R. E. Whalen, notably). This analysis assumes that there are two basic mechanisms physiologically given. The first, labeled the "sexual arousal mechanism," refers to the fact that touching the genitals brings pleasurable arousal. As this stimulation gets more intense, the second mechanism takes over, namely the convulsive upheaval of orgasm (which is termed, for the male, the intromissive and ejaculatory mechanism).

Now the mechanism of orgasm is stereotyped and largely involuntary. But the sexual arousal mechanism, in human beings, is very changeable and conditionable. Through conditioning, the arousal which stimulation of the genitals brings can be evoked by touching other parts of the body and above all by imagination and other thought processes. The context in which sexual stimulation occurs will determine the other emotional responses that become associated with it. It is worth mentioning that Albert Bandura and Richard Walters (in their study, *Adolescent Aggression*) found that youths who had a history of conflict with their parents, associated sexual arousal with aggressive feeling. Among other youths, sexual arousal was coupled with tender feelings.

The final link in learning sexual behavior takes place during adolescence when a boy or girl discovers that when arousal reaches a given pitch it triggers the second, orgasmic mechanism. As this link grows firmly established, sexual arousal, from being a pleasurable state in itself, becomes a foretaste of something much better. Hence it may thereafter be felt to be frustrating if it is not concluded with orgasm.

Once sexual arousal is thus associated with imagination and with the mind, cultural influences (whether friends, art, comics, advertisements or entertainment) can condition one to feel sexual arousal even *before* the relevant stimulus takes place. A boy will learn to expect that holding the hand of a girl his own age will arouse him sexually, though he knows that the hands of his aunts have no such magic. The fact that one can induce or reduce sexual arousal by taking thought means that it is at least partly a matter of volition, not compulsion. The cookbooks on sexual technique recognize this when they recommend that a man who wants to delay orgasm during intercourse, in the interests of his partner's pleasure, should divert his mind to other, non-sexual matters.

Sexual appetite, then, is a habit by which one has *learned* to expect pleasurable arousal and orgasm in certain kinds of situations. (The innate component is the *capacity* for arousal and orgasm.) The emotions and imaginings that accompany sexual appetite—tenderness, shame, aggression, or whatever—are inseparable from it. D. H. Lawrence fulminated against "sex in the head." But if sex in the head were somehow eliminated, sexual desire and behavior would largely disappear. For human sex is sustained and directed much more by stimuli the individual has learned to perceive as arousing, and by his own self-directed imagining, than by physiology.

Though we haven't the evidence to be sure, it seems that those religious people who take vows of chastity and consider masturbation a sin, achieve a life in which sexual arousal is minimal, and the orgasmic mechanism falls into more or less permanent disuse. And they are none the worse for it. On the hypothesis that sex is a biological "need" like hunger or thirst, one has to infer complicated processes of repression and sublimation to account for this. But on the appetite theory we can suppose either that sexual arousal has not been conditioned much to stimuli other than direct touching of the genitals, in the first place; or that through the discipline of their way of life, these people have undergone a massive de-conditioning so that arousal now comes from very few stimuli other than directly tactile ones. At the same time, their commitment to their beliefs makes them mentally restructure many stimuli which would "normally" arouse them, so that they evoke other kinds of emotion. A priest may habitually *see* attractive women as children of God in need of forgiveness, rather than as potential bed-mates.

Whether or not one goes the whole way with the theory that human sexual behavior is basically an appetite that is learned, there's no doubt it is a much needed corrective to the theory of biological need. It is in harmony with much everyday observation, and it has certain social implications. According to the moralists, our present-day society is obsessed with sex, and in their view of course this is a bad thing. Certainly novelists, film makers, dramatists and advertisers (not to mention dress designers) now have great freedom to exploit stimuli that are sexually arousing. Defenders of this freedom commonly base their case upon the "biological need" theory of sex. Their argument goes something like this. Sexual stimulation cannot make people any more sexually motivated than they are by nature, because the strength of each person's sexual drive is biologically determined. On the other hand, freedom of sexual expression in society will tend to disinhibit those in whom the sexual instinct is repressed or suppressed. But this is beneficial because healthy living demands that our basic instincts should be satisfied. If we bottle up our sex energies, they go bad on us.

The "appetite" theory leads to a rather different assessment. What we are doing is cultivating our sexual appetites by steadily extending the variety of stimuli that provoke sexual arousal, and by sustaining this arousal through filling our minds with sexual imagery and thought. Biology may set limits (both upper and lower) to how far we can develop these appetites; but within these limits the possibilities are wide. As a society we appear to have decided to maximize them.

Obviously it does not follow from the appetite theory that it is wrong to cultivate our sexual appetites. That must be decided on other grounds (though it does seem silly to cultivate them freely, and at the same time deny them satisfaction). A case could be made for saying that, provided we take suitable measures to control birth, sex is a better appetite to cultivate than others like power or the itch to interfere in the lives of others. But the point is that our defense of sexual freedom will have to be on other grounds than biological need.

A more important issue raised by the appetite theory is the nature of the emotions we judge appropriate to sexual arousal. A glance at the various cultural influences at work—from advertising and novels, to religious tracts and sermons—suggests a whole string of emotions that are currently associated with sex: desire for social status and success; aggression and cruelty; pride in skillful performance; self-contempt, fear and guilt; aesthetic feeling; delight in the forbidden; inferiority; curiosity; and even mystical experience. And there are some influences (Kinsey?) which tend to separate sex from any other kind of emotional response and make it a thing apart from other aspects of living.

If sex is to be fully human and personal, then it ought to be linked with affection, tenderness and awareness of the feelings of others. This, one may suppose, is the normal outcome of a warmly affectionate and reasonably permissive upbringing. In any case, the more sex is associated with fear, guilt, aggression and the rest, the less it will be integrated with affection. Rather than lament the fact that sexual appetite is now being encouraged, we might more profitably spend our time trying to ensure that the emotions that are integrated with it are the ones we approve of. To condition sexual arousal to moral feelings of guilt and obligation may destroy the ties with affection as effectively as conditioning it to cruelty or disgust.

We hear much of the "public concern" over the sexual morality of the young. Yet when you listen to what the young themselves have to say, in surveys and personal conversations, you find that a great many of them are in fact rejecting traditional morality precisely in order to maintain and affirm this coalescence of sexual desire and affection. As they see it, to hedge sexual behavior, but not affection, with rules is to push the two apart. For me, this attitude revives the faded hope that one day we may have a society in which the social influences surrounding us all conspire to tie sex and affection inextricably together.

Then perhaps the moralists and the press will give up writing about it, because nobody will be interested in reading what they have to say.

## *About the Authors*

Ernest Becker has taught cultural anthropology at Berkeley and San Francisco State. He is the author of *Angel in Armor.*

Paul Bindrim led the first nude group marathon. He practices psychotherapy in Hollywood, California.

Norman O. Brown is professor of classics at Wesleyan University. He is the author of *Life Against Death* and *Love's Body.*

Tom Burke appears regularly in *Esquire* and the *New York Sunday Times* entertainment section.

Jeremy Bugler is a British writer, formerly of the staff of *New Society.*

Robert Craft is the first American to have conducted both of Alban Berg's operas—*Wozzeck* and *Lulu.* He has collaborated with Igor Stravinsky on six books, the latest being *Retrospectives and Conclusions.*

Dr. Leslie Farber is Director of Therapy at Austen Riggs Center, Inc. in Stockbridge, Massachusetts. His essays have appeared in *Commentary* and *Harper's.*

Dan Greenburg is one of several authors of *Oh! Calcutta!* He also wrote *How to be a Jewish Mother.*

E. J. Hobsbawm teaches European social and economic history at the University of London. He is the author of *The Age of Revolution: 1789–1848, Primitive Rebels,* and *Labouring Men: Studies in the History of Labour.*

Cris Hodenfield is the author of *Rock 70.*

Dorothy Kalins is a New York free-lance writer.

Craig Karpel is a contributing editor at *Esquire* and *US,* majoring in pop culture.

Susan Lydon is a contributing editor at *Ramparts*.

Joe Mancini is a New York writer.

Herbert Marcuse wrote *Reason and Revolution, Eros and Civilization,* and *One Dimensional Man.* He is professor of philosophy at the University of California at San Diego.

Peter Michaelson has taught English at Notre Dame and the University of Wyoming. His book, *The Aesthetics of Pornography,* was published by Herder and Herder.

Thomas Nagel teaches philosophy at Princeton.

Philip Nobile is a former editor of the *Commonweal* and currently press critic for the *National Catholic Reporter.*

George Steiner is Fellow and Director of English Studies at Churchill College, Cambridge University. He wrote *Tolstoy or Dostoevsky, The Death of Tragedy,* and *Language and Silence.*

Kenneth Tynan is a former literary manager of the British National Theatre and organizer of *Oh! Calcutta!*

Ross Wetzsteon is an associate editor of the *Village Voice.*

Derek Wright is a lecturer in psychology at Leicester University in England.

Charles Winick is a professor of sociology at the City University of New York and the author of *The New People: Desexualization of American Life.*